NEW QUILTS:
Interpretations & Innovations

QUILT NATIONAL

West Chester, Pennsylvania 19380

ACKNOWLEDGMENTS

Quilt National wishes to express its gratitude to the following individuals and organizations whose contributions are too numerous to count and too great to measure:

Pamela S. Parker, Executive Director, The Dairy Barn Southeastern Ohio Cultural Arts Center, Athens, Ohio

Hilary Morrow Fletcher, Quilt National '89 Coordinator

The Dairy Barn Board of Directors

The staff of the Dairy Barn Southeastern Ohio Cultural Arts Center

FAIRFIELD PROCESSING CORPORATION, makers of Poly-fil® fiber products and batting material, Danbury, Connecticut

The Ohio Arts Council

Peter Schiffer, Schiffer Publishing, Ltd., West Chester, Pennsylvania

The many volunteers from the Athens community who participate in this project

The local businesses who contribute goods and services

The Quilt National artists without whom there could be no Quilt National

EDITOR: Nancy Roe
DESIGN: Mark Johnson, Brannon Graphics
PHOTOGRAPHY: Brian Blauser, unless otherwise noted

Cover: *Glad Rags*, Joyce Marquess Carey, Madison, Wisconsin—see page 73

This book may be purchased from Quilt National or the publisher.
Please include $2.00 for postage and handling.
Try your bookstore first.

NEW QUILTS:
Interpretations & Innovations

From the Dairy Barn's Executive Director

As Quilt National rounds the corner of its first decade, it is only fitting to reflect on its beginnings and contemplate its future.

The Quilt National '79 exhibition was a first. It was the first juried competition for contemporary quilt artists. It was the first major exhibition at the Dairy Barn, and it was my first show as executive director of the Dairy Barn Southeastern Ohio Cultural Arts Center.

Quilt National established a new vehicle for the contemporary quilt artist to exhibit his/her work. The goal was then, as it still is, to promote contemporary quilting as an art form. It was an ambitious project that a very dedicated group of volunteers undertook ten years ago. Emerging quilt artists Nancy Crow, Françoise Barnes and others established a national network of quilters to let them know about this new show that would highlight the BEST in the field of contemporary quiltmaking. That first year, 190 artists submitted 390 works. Of those, 56 pieces were selected. The response to this first exhibition was overwhelming. People could not get enough of these new works of art.

Over the last decade, this biennial Quilt National has become the standard by which other exhibitions are measured. The exhibition quilts are selected by top designers, museum directors and quilt artists. The works chosen continue to be fresh, innovative and boundless in the way they stretch our imagination, and I am constantly awed by their design, craftsmanship and subject matter. It has been exciting to watch the evolution of the contemporary quilt over the last ten years and to chart the interest this exhibition has generated worldwide.

The 1989 Quilt National jurors had the very difficult task of selecting 82 works from 1,156 entries submitted by 560 artists from Australia, Brazil, Canada, Denmark, England, France, Ireland, Israel, Japan, New Zealand, Norway, Switzerland, West Germany and throughout the United States.

Quilt National '83 toured some small museums and galleries in the United States after its opening at the Dairy Barn. The 1985 show also went on tour, but this time some of the larger galleries and museums were included, such as American Craft in New York. In 1987, Quilt National made its international debut. After opening at the Dairy Barn, the show went to Washington, D.C., and New York City and then traveled to Japan for a six-month tour. The show delighted 33,000 enthusiastic visitors in twelve days at the Daimaru Department Store exhibition hall in Tokyo before moving on to five more cities in Japan.

In 1989-1991, this sixth biennial Quilt National will once again delight audiences from Maine to Alaska and will travel throughout Japan.

In Japan, the artist is a highly respected and revered individual, recognized for valued contributions to the culture and heritage of society. The staff and volunteers of the Dairy Barn have that same kind of respect and admiration for the many artists who have entrusted their works to us to share with the world. I would like to thank the 1,738 artists who have entered a total of 4,773 quilts over the last ten years for allowing us to view, exhibit and enjoy their creations. Whether accepted into a particular show or not, each artist has contributed something to the growth and development of contemporary quilting as an art form. As for the many thousands more who will enter in the future, I encourage them to design and create, stretching our definition of the quilt and continuing to delight us with their works, as we enter the next decade of Quilt National!

Pamela S. Parker
Executive Director

INTRODUCTION
TO QUILT NATIONAL '89

December 1988: The 80 works juried into Quilt National '89 have been shipped to the Dairy Barn Southeastern Ohio Cultural Arts Center to be photograped for this catalogue. Hilary Fletcher, Quilt National coordinator, has placed them, protected by unbleached muslin, in the cool storage space carved out of what was once a 200-foot-long hayloft.

Even covered, some quilt edges show and catch the eye. When Hilary, full of delight in her impresario role, pulls a cover back, a blaze of color lights up the white wallboard space, whetting the viewer's eye and mind for the moment when Quilt National '89 will be installed in the Dairy Barn's exhibition space and fully accessible.

. . . .

This sixth biennial Quilt National continues to evidence trends that had their genesis in 1979's first exhibit. A decade later, the vast majority of the works selected are by women and men who consider themselves professional artists. Most have had formal training. Others are self-taught, but far removed from the Sunday painter category. Their work has been selected from nearly 1,160 entries from around the globe.

These artists continually challenge themselves, strive to expand their visions, stretch their boundaries, take risks. More and more are creating "fiber paint" by dyeing, painting and piecing fabric and employing elements from fiberglass mesh to beads and stuffed, embroidered forms. Some works are encrusted and thick with layers of elements. Many incorporate both machine and hand stitching, machine and hand appliqué.

Inspiration for the Quilt National artists comes from many sources, ranging from Nature—tornadoes, seasons, weather-worn tiles—to social issues—political prisoners, race relations, aging, male-female relationships. Musicians from Mozart to Joe Cocker inspire. Art movements from impressionism, cubism, art deco, op art and post-modernism play a role. Cultures from American Indian to Mexican to Arabian to Japanese set off sparks. Traditional quilt patterns like Log Cabin, Drunkard's Path and Chinese Coins still influence.

Intensely serious about what they are doing, many of the artists nevertheless display wit and even outrageous humor. In Cynthia Lambert and Janet Lorini's "St. Irving and the Archangels," an imaginary saint flies "around Pittsburgh sprinkling good fortune on hard-working, talented and humble artists." In "Tropical New York," Susan Shie has captured the gaudy, bawdy, weirdly wonderful city that attracts and repels at one-and-the-same time.

One artist's husband told her she was "possessed by quilting." It's a phrase that might well apply to all Quilt National artists. Several give reasons: "It is truly like painting with fabrics," Patty Hawkins writes. Natasha Kempers-Cullen speaks of the "energizing" that comes from "working with such familiar materials in a serious way." Jane Sassaman finds that "these 'soft paintings' satisfy the draftsman, the craftsman and the artist in me." Suma Smith delights in a medium that "erases mindset barriers so often associated with other forms of art."

Studying Quilt National '89 and contemplating what one decade has brought in the art quilt field, viewers can only revel in the works and look forward to all the next decade holds.

About the Jurors

Photo provided by juror.

Chris Wolf Edmonds, Lawrence, Kansas: As a self-taught quiltmaker with more than 20 years of experience, Chris Edmonds has earned an international reputation. She has won numerous awards and commissions, and her work has appeared in many publications. In addition to serving as a juror for several major shows, she teaches and lectures on quilt design. Her work ranges from appliqué picture quilts to more abstract pieces dealing with illusory space, form, light and motion.

Photo provided by juror.

Bernard Kester, Los Angeles, California: Bernard Kester has been an active participant in crafts and design programs and organizations for the past 25 years. He is currently acting dean of the College of Fine Arts at the University of California, Los Angeles. He served as a juror for the International Textile Fair '87 in Kyoto, Japan, and has been a guest curator for many art museums in the United States. His textiles have been widely exhibited, and he has been the recipient of numerous national awards.

Photo by Elaine F. Keenan.

Yvonne Porcella, Modesto, California: In addition to being among the most widely recognized of today's quilt artists, Yvonne Porcella lectures and teaches throughout the world. She was an invited instructor for the First Australian Quilt Symposium, and has also taught in Japan and Germany. She is the author of several books, including *YVONNE PORCELLA: A Colorful Book*, which documents some of the ways in which she uses color to create visual and emotional excitement.

Statements from the Quilt National '89 Jurors

Chris Wolf Edmonds

Minimizing the Risk of Rejection

Entering any competition should be done with conscious concern for the considerable risk involved: the risk of rejection. As artists and craftsmen we want our personal artistic expressions as well as our practiced and perfected technique to be recognized and admired by our peers and by those whose opinions we respect. We aspire to see our work accepted as part of a group of works which are chosen to represent the best, whether it is a local guild show or an international competition. In order to maximize the possibilities for acceptance, entries should be made with our eyes wide open, with knowledge of the criteria for any particular show, and with the greatest possible objectivity about our own work.

In 1988 I judged or juried three major national quilt shows, including Quilt National '89. The others were more traditional shows, although each had categories for original design. I saw many of the same quilts entered into all three shows, and many of the top award winners in one show did not win prizes or were totally rejected from another. Each show was in a different part of the country, each had a different set of judges (except for me), and each had different formats and different criteria for awards or selection.

One of the most important factors to consider is the focus of the particular show you wish to enter. Quilt National states on its entry form that it is "dedicated to promoting the contemporary quilt as an art form." It goes on to state that "All works must be an original design of the entrant, not a copy of a traditional design nor a variation on the original design of another artist." If the quilt you have made and wish to enter in competition is a traditional pattern, no matter how spectacular your color and value arrangement, or how perfect your construction techniques, you run a high risk of rejection if you enter it in Quilt National because it will not meet the criteria for original design. There are other shows which have special categories for traditional quilts which will give you a much better chance for acceptance.

In the world of contemporary quiltmaking, many of the best known artists are also teachers. Taking a workshop from one of these artists can be a very rewarding learning experience. It may be just what you need to gain the courage to branch out into original design. Often, however, pieces started as workshop projects bear so great an influence from the teacher/artist that they, too, would be high risks for rejection in Quilt National since they are merely "variations on the original design of another artist." Likewise, design and color exercises based on the work of artists from other media, such as Vasarely or Escher or Albers, are not what Quilt National is looking for. While these exercises may be valuable in helping to develop your own sense of color and design, they do not make appropriate entries in a show or category which requires original design.

Creating a work that is original, appealing, innovative and fresh may still not assure acceptance. The work must also be presented to the jury or judges in such a way that they recognize its beauty and genius. In a show such as Quilt National that is juried by slides, excellent photography becomes absolutely essential. This fact has been stressed by show coordinators and juries for years, but they are still subjected to over- and under-exposed slides and poorly displayed pieces which cannot possibly be fairly assessed.

It takes a great deal of courage to enter your work, your own personal expression, into competition. Ultimately, you have to be personally satisfied with your own work, to be gratified when others recognize and admire it, and to persevere when it is ignored or rejected.

Bernard Kester

New Images Out of an Old Tradition

The motives and sources in the making of quilts have changed over many years of history as family and cultural traditions have evolved and diversified. In large measure, quilts were the creation of useful products from a collective impulse and activity reflecting familiar and community values expressed in conventionalized images and patterns that yet maintain well known associations and symbols (Log Cabin, Sawtooth, Feathered Star, among others.) Narrative, commemorative and decorative functions have lifted the quilt beyond its fundamental role as a bedcover.

When the quilt began to be considered for its aesthetic worth and became a vehicle for individual creative expression, new freedoms in design were explored, new images developed out of old traditions, and alternative reference sources tapped. Creative invention has taken place primarily on the quilt surface, while the construction which has identified the quilt traditionally as a "sandwich of fabric layers secured by stitching" has remained largely unchanged. Most often viewed on a plane, the quilt is a two-dimensional surface that easily adapts to design that is graphic in nature. Seldom is it so deeply quilted as to be perceived as a relief.

Although the quilt was part of the fiber movement in America that began its vigorous and expansive development in the 1960s, it has remained apart. Stitchery, soft sculpture and fabric collage shared new energies in common with the quilt. Yet the quilt has retained its independence primarily because of its conservative structure. The fiber movement as a whole fostered experimental pursuits utilizing non-traditional materials and processes, and prompted expressive design in quilts while attracting more artists to this medium. An increased program of regional and national contemporary crafts exhibitions and fairs has encouraged greater opportunity for experimental quiltmakers to become accepted outside their communities, QUILT NATIONAL being the most important among these.

Opportunity for worldwide travel in recent years has increased, and awareness of the arts of native and primitive cultures has prompted the appropriation of images and patterns from those sources into various fields of the visual arts, including quilts. Certain entries submitted this year appeared to be uninspired transcriptions from the Navajo Two Gray Hills and Yei style rugs. Restored interest in American folk art has witnessed the renewal of certain motifs reconfigured into contemporary terms. Abstract and figural painting has served to inspire quiltmakers to undertake similar optical, narrative and pictorial problems. It is in this range of work that many ideas from painting have been successfully transformed to quilting materials and methods. The recent pattern painters have inspired the layering of pattern on pattern apparent among the most inventive, complex and successful works in this exhibition.

Diverse sources of reference, particularly from outside the quiltmakers' tradition, have built this QUILT NATIONAL into a rich contemporary exhibition that is art.

Yvonne Porcella

Reflections on the Jurying Process

The entry form for Quilt National states that the competition is dedicated to promoting the contemporary quilt as an art form and that submitted work will be judged on originality, technique and craftsmanship. As 1989 jurors, we were instructed to emphasize the most innovative and exciting work being done by quiltmakers throughout the world. We viewed slides of 1,156 works and selected only those quilts which we felt best interpreted the rules and fulfilled the intentions of the competition.

The color catalogs of Quilt National serve as a documented history of the development of contemporary quilting as an art form. It is to the previous show catalogs I would like to refer in my discussion of the selection of the 1989 show. A survey of the selections since 1979 shows clearly how the art quiltmaker is developing. Increasingly more quilts reflect the personality of the maker. The skill of defining the medium is evidenced in refined images. The artists have progressed rapidly in a decade from 19th century block-geometric quilts into the contemporary arena. Many artists today utilize modern tools to aid in the construction. This reflects the change of our 1980's lifestyle as well as how we see quilts. Quilts included in Quilt National are usually intended by the maker to be viewed on the wall as works of art. The original premise in the mind of the artist is to make an artistic statement, not a bedspread.

Since 1979, the selection of quilts in Quilt National has been made by a panel of jurors. Therefore the resultant exhibit reflects the preferences of these individuals and the panel as a group. Each juror brings his or her personal expertise and judgment to the process. In the judging process, the quilts are viewed by slides: thus, the level of photography becomes a contributing factor in the selection. The entry form instructs entrants to use high-quality photography. If the artist personally takes the picture, he or she may not be aware of imperfections of lighting or composition—and may know too well what the picture should show. The artist must give the jurors the best possible image of the work, or the work will be ignored.

Quilt National aspires to showcase the newest and best of the submitted entries. As the judging progressed, the show seemed to build itself. Those quilts with strong design effects became so powerful they almost had a voice which called out—for example, the humor in Patty Hawkins's "Cactus People" and the strong emotion of Cherry Partee's quilt "The Epiphany of Joanna Burden." Partee's quilt utilizes a traditional repetitive block, but the overall effect of the figure form within the composition is sure to generate comment from those who view this work.

In the jury process, we became aware of how a title reflects the artist's statement. Each piece was known to us by an entry number and title. As I write this essay, the titles help revisualize the piece: for instance, "Putting the Guise to Bed" provokes a clear image of Darcy Usilton's concept of just who those "guys" are. Robin Schwalb's title "Rosetta Stone" also easily conveys the content of her quilt.

There were many quilts submitted that did not receive acceptance for this 1989 show. These quilts were not necessarily inferior, but they did not project a unique expression to this year's

jurors. A quilt can be a technically correct design exercise, but if the personality of the artist is not projected, that quilt may well be eliminated. It is expected that the artist have the fundamental skills of color usage and the technical ability to execute the design. The quilt must show the development of the artist's concept; the quilt must have substance and draw the viewer in.

The question always arises of why jurors select two quilts by the same artist rather than quilts by a greater number of artists. As Quilt National jurors, we selected what we perceived to be the best pieces for the exhibition. Names of the artists are not revealed until the jurors have made their final selection, and it was only then that we became aware of duplications. The two entries by Cherry Partee clearly illustrate how two images by the same artist may be accepted: "Long Distance Call" and "The Epiphany of Joanna Burden" are both strong pieces reflective of a sensitive artist. Even the colors and fabrics are entirely different in these two entries, and both are excellent examples of the development of a theme.

Again referring to the previous catalogs, we can illustrate how Quilt National has shown the development of individual artists. In 1981 Judith Dingle submitted a quilt titled "Windows" with red to pink stripes appearing as the background behind blue attic window blocks. The illusion was there of viewing through a window. In 1989, Dingle's entry hints at the same theme, but now she effectively uses the negative space between her three-dimensional forms to give the illusion of a pieced block. Dingle has made the background behind her blocks a part of her quilt: the viewer looks through the transparent material to imagine the form as a flat quilt.

The 1989 Quilt National exhibit contains works that will generate strong responses from the viewer. It was not the intent to choose controversial quilts for this show, however, but to select new and exciting work. I believe that, in order for the contemporary quilt to be viewed as art, a good show should provoke comments from its audience.

I am very excited about this show and suggest that those whose work was not accepted try again next time. I also urge them to look at this 1989 show and study their own work. It is only by knowing where everyone else is in quiltmaking that artists can push their own work further. Many of the artists included this year are new to Quilt National and have not shown in previous years. I applaud them if they were eliminated from past shows and persevered to try again.

Judith Dingle
Toronto, Ontario, Canada
Reconstruction
Dupioni silk, fiberglass screen, wooden rods, rubber grommets
and cotton. 32″ x 60″, photographed against a white background.

Recently, I have been exploring three-dimensional mixed media
textile constructions that relate to the graphic imagery of my
previous work. While alluding to the quilt format, these wall
pieces, by virtue of their construction and materials, extend the
traditional definition of the quilt. Traditionally, the pieced quilt
has been composed of blocks that interact with one another. By
treating the block as a separate stuffed unit, I am drawing
attention to its singular nature without denying its role in the
overall larger image. These individual blocks, though separated,
are held together structurally with a gridwork of vertical screen
and horizontal rods. In this way, the quilt's elements are
fragmented, redefined and restored to create a new form and
meaning. This transformation and synthesis is a major concern in
my current work.

**AWARD FOR MOST
INNOVATIVE USE OF THE MEDIUM**

Jan Maher
Greensboro, North Carolina
Reflections IV
Cotton, cotton sateen, rayon and gold lamé.
Machine pieced and quilted. 68″ x 76″

In this quilt I pushed the idea of being able to see
into windows of another building. Since the view
is not usually clear, I overlaid a printed fabric
with black cotton voile to give the effect of
looking through a window screen.

Barbara Oliver Hartman
Flower Mound, Texas
Safari Blizzard
Cotton fabric, rayon cording, polyester batting.
Machine pieced, hand appliquéd and hand
quilted using both metallic and cotton threads.
74″ x 52″

I was interested in the colors working right to left
and left to right, and in mixing colors not
normally used together. The title suggests
inconsistency or contradiction. The quilt depicts
the turmoil, contrasts, beauty and division of
South Africa.

Ruth B. McDowell
Winchester, Massachusetts
The Yellow Maple
Cottons and linens. Machine pieced and hand quilted. 86″ x 68″
From a private collection.

October in a New England wood.

Dorle Stern-Straeter
München, West Germany
Arabia
Cotton, silk and chintz. Crazy technique, hand quilted. 70" x 61"

From 1983-1988 I lived in Saudi Arabia. There I studied Arabic patterns. "Arabia" is made of crazy-triangle blocks in an Arabic pattern.

Joan Schulze
Sunnyvale, California
Old Koi, Old Pond
Various fabrics, including silk, cotton, nylon, netting and lamé.
Some fabrics dyed and printed; hand and machine stitched.
37″ x 27″

Life has always been my subject—a running commentary on
day-to-day events as minor as skywatching or as major as an
investigation of contemporary marriage. The complexities of life
seem best expressed in fabric which endures so many magical
changes—dyeing, painting, cutting, piecing—a perfect metaphor
for life. I find it impossible to separate the two.

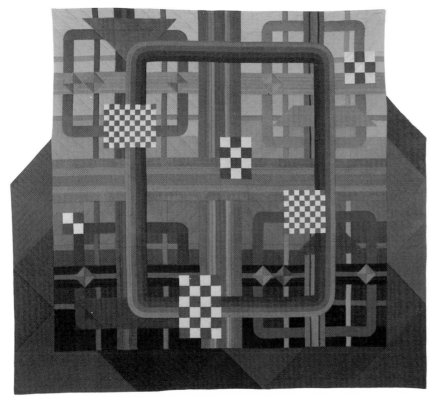

Jane Reeves
Canton, Ohio
Post Modern XIII
Hand-dyed cotton. Machine pieced and hand quilted. 80″ x 70″

My quilt designs are abstract and focus on such formal issues as color, shape, line and their use to create illusions of space and movement. They do not represent material reality, nor are they literally about anything tangible: they are visual revelations, momentary glimpses, flashes of meaning.

Tafi Brown
East Alstead, New Hampshire
Trees IV: All Seasons
Cyanotype prints on cotton. Machine pieced and quilted, hand appliquéd. 76″ x 46″

This quilt is from a series—on which I am currently at work—that deals with New England trees and landscapes and seasonal changes. I like working with the concrete visual image and then the visual ambiguities that develop when composing a whole piece. I like working with dualities and hidden meanings and messages, both obvious and not obvious.

Irene Kahmann
Groebenzell, West Germany
Captured Light
Hand-painted and hand-dyed silks and cottons. Machine pieced
and hand quilted. 72″ x 58″

I paint all silk material myself using only primary colors and
black. So I prepare a whole set of a certain polychromatic color-
combinations for one quilt. In addition, to obtain more movement on the material, I draw and paint lines and structures on
prepared silk. Then, using uni-colored as well as the painted silk
of my special color combination, I cut pieces and strips and
compose them together. Therefore all lines are completed before
the cutting and sewing are done.

Marguerite Malwitz
Brookfield, Connecticut
Desert Dusk
Cottons and blends, silk, satin, cotton and metallic threads. Tie-dyed, hand and machine pieced, hand quilted. 53″ x 44″

"Desert Dusk" was inspired by the simple lines and complex color changes in the Arizona desert and also by a visit to the Desert Botanical Gardens in Phoenix. Further inspiration came from Isaiah 35:1—"The desert and the parched land will be glad; the wilderness will rejoice and blossom."

Nancy Erickson
Missoula, Montana
The Visitation
Velvet, satin and cotton fabrics. Hand painted and glued and machine appliquéd on a painted background. 89″ x 72″
Supported in part by a fellowship from the Montana Arts Council, an agency of State Government.

This work, which pictures a real incident (in which a full-grown pet pig joined the pleasant conversations on the living room couch), is really about a future in which animal presence is more widely acknowledged. The capybara, a 150-pound rodent from South America, has been substituted for the pig.

Natasha Kempers-Cullen
Bowdoinham, Maine
Daydream at Dusk
Cotton fabrics hand painted with Procion dyes. Machine pieced,
machine and hand quilted. 48″ x 29″

This piece started very spontaneously. I simply wanted to work
wet on wet and observe the effects of overlaying colors. As the
painting developed, the structure of the quilt became more static,
more defined. I painted nine separate panels which I then pieced
together. The window-like images are fundamental to all of my
work. The question is: Am I outside, looking in, or inside, looking
out? Am I ever a real part of the situation or is there always a kind
of wall of separation around me?

Linda S. Perry
Lexington, Massachusetts
Thoughts of Karen
Cottons, silks (some hand dyed) and rayon. Hand appliquéd,
machine pieced and machine quilted. 90″ x 50″

After a spate of mauve and vague quilts, this was my leap into
chroma. I began designing the first block with Art Deco and serial
imagery in mind. This design was then altered and simplified to
yield a set of blocks that are related but not identical. When the
quilt was completed, it reminded me of a walk I had taken with a
friend many years ago, and so I call it "Thoughts of Karen."

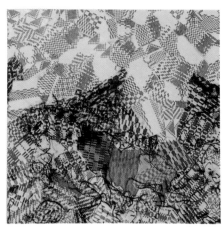

detail

Carol D. Westfall
Nutley, New Jersey
Crazy Quilt I
Computer-generated weave structure printouts, paint, fiberglass screening. Layered and hand stitched. 42″ x 60″

This piece is part of a series of "Crazy Quilts" which pay homage to the American tradition of piecing odd scraps of fabric together and to 20th century technology in terms of computer-generated weave structures. The series began initially in box form with a silk grid inside each box. These were metaphors for the grid on the computer screen which aids in creating patterns.

Emiko Toda Loeb
New York, New York
Taketorimonogatari ("The Bamboo Cutter" Folktale)
Japanese antique cotton fabrics (Meiji period), new Japanese
cotton and Indonesian batik. Crazy quilt with machine piecing
and quilting done by hand with sashiko stitch technique using
natural dye thread. 56" x 73"

This is a crazy quilt only because there is no traditional block
pattern replicated into a grid. Nevertheless the diagonal and
vertical lines create a strong organizational sense closely related
to traditional pattern ideas.

Sharon Johnson Clark
Portage, Michigan
Ins and Outs
Cottons and blends. Machine pieced, hand quilted and hand appliquéd. 48″ x 48″
From a private collection.

This is the second of a series of pieces utilizing strips, occasional tucks, miniature blocks and stars and many "windows" of interest. The pieces are very structured in background—with interest concentrated on value, depth and intricate surprises.

Barbara Lydecker Crane
Lexington, Massachusetts
Internal Map
Cotton fabrics, some of which are hand dyed or hand painted; seed pearl beads, mother-of-pearl birds and fish. Machine and hand pieced, hand quilted with cotton and metallic threads. 62″ x 62″
From a private collection.

I made this quilt in wonderment and appreciation for the mysteries of nature. The grid format refers to the apparent sameness of the underlying structure of all animate life, while the painted extremities of the animals give tribute to the elegant and varied articulation which nature builds on this repeating structure.

Kaoru Kawaguchi
Kumamoto, Japan
Nagareru
Cotton fabric. Machine pieced and hand quilted. 75″ x 86″

"Nagareru" means stream or long continuous series of things. I am alive now in the endless stream of time and space. I want to keep on living as brightly and freely as an innocent stream of water flowing into another wider stream.

Carol Jessen
Applegate, California
Ice Cream Parlor Chairs
Xerography on paper, voile, other fabrics and flannel batting.
Appliquéd, shadow appliquéd and hand quilted using widely-spaced backstitching to make quilting invisible on front surface.
29" x 40"

One aspect of traditional quiltmaking which I have always liked is the repetition of components—usually block designs—to create pattern and rhythm. In this piece I have used as a repeat motif an image created and replicated instantly by technological means not usually associated with quiltmaking. The repetition of the image out of its ordinary context makes it more abstract.

Sue Benner
Dallas, Texas
Summer
Cottons and blends, some commercially printed
and others painted with pigments and dyes.
Machine pieced by artist, hand quilted by Julie
Barnes. 73″ x 73″

"Summer" is one in a series of quilts about the
seasons in which I've used both painted and
printed fabrics. The arrangement of color and
quilting depicts intense sun, deep shade, radiant
heat and soothing waves of water. The Texas
summer is a relentless season.

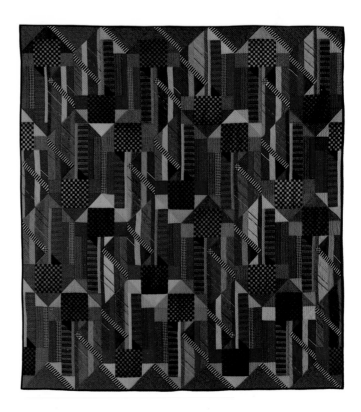

Sharon Heidingsfelder
Little Rock, Arkansas
Encore, Encore
Cotton fabrics, some hand dyed or silkscreened.
Machine pieced by the artist and hand quilted by
Roumilda Hurn, Pocahontas, Arkansas. 70″ x 76″

I design my quilts by repeating a single block
motif. Arranging and rearranging the blocks
produces interesting shapes. After choosing one
of the combinations, I then use strip-piecing,
hand-dyed fabrics or silkscreened prints to add
more interest to some of the shapes. I always use
a black-and-white piece of fabric in my quilts.

Susan Shie
Wooster, Ohio
Tropical New York
Stuffed and sewn forms attached to many types of painted fabric, beads, shells, plastic clay, plastic toy animals. Hand embroidered, hand pieced, hand quilted. 95″ x 84″

Tropical New York—it's a far cry from my usual Ohio landscape! The alligators in the sewers; the subways becoming snakes; Buffy the parrot who lived at the top of my apartment building; my friends swooning over the sexy waiter; my family's visit when Jimmy sprained his ankle at South Street Seaport and limped through the subways at rush hour; the pick-pockets in the crystal shop who got chased away empty handed; our ad-hoc voice-meditation class at PS 1's International Artists Studios Program! It was briefly my neighborhood and this is a diary of my adventures there—the last in a three-quilt series called "Ms. Ohio Attacks New York." My new hero is a female Godzilla!! New York does that to you!

David Walker
Cincinnati, Ohio
The Enchanted Land of the Lotus Eaters
Cottons and blends, control-bleached and dyed fabrics, beads,
sequins and fabric paint. Machine pieced and appliquéd.
88" x 60"

The time and space which we occupy is such a comfortable place.
We are anesthetized by that which we call reality, often feeling
powerless over our circumstances and believing that we must
"react to" rather than "create" them. We no longer remember
how to take charge of the present moment nor how to create our
own special reality of peace and light. We are in many places at
the same time, but still we only bear witness to the reality that we
are able to know and experience with our senses. Too often this
reality becomes our only truth. There is so much more, but we
have eaten of the Lotus Flower, and under its hypnotic spell, we
mistakenly feel safe and serene and do not realize the prison we
have made for ourselves.

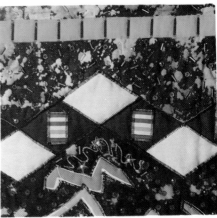

detail

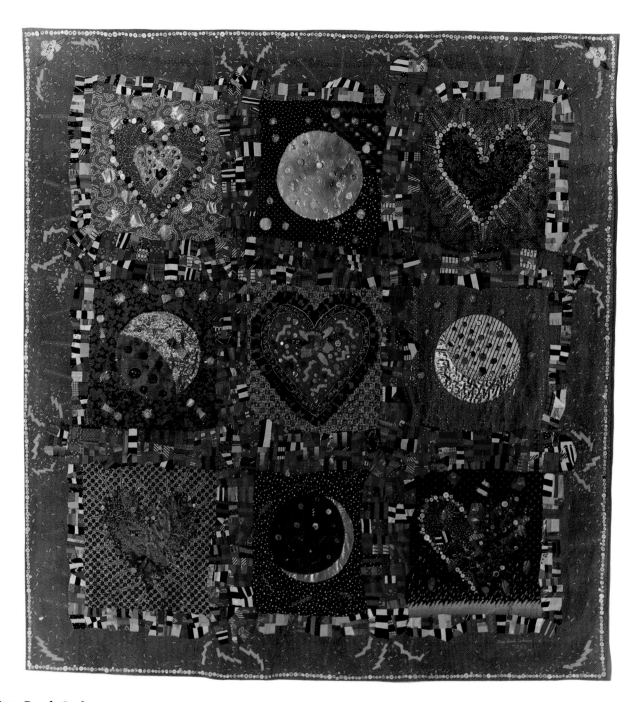

Jane Burch Cochran
Rabbit Hash, Kentucky
Phases of the Heart, Phases of the Moon
Assorted fabrics, including pieces from an antique beaded dress
of black net owned by a Kentucky woman, painted canvas, beads,
buttons and shells. Machine pieced, with hand appliquéd and
hand stitched beadwork. 100″ x 105″

With the many esoteric meanings in art today, I enjoy using two
common symbols—the heart and the moon—that everyone
relates to in some way. The heart represents the physical and
emotional qualities and includes heart of gold, heartburn,
sweetheart, purple heart and broken heart. The moon represents
the spiritual qualities and includes full moon, new moon and
waxing and waning moons. The copper-colored moon also
represents a "wet moon": when one point is higher than the
other, the moon "bowl" will overflow and rain. The silver
crescent represents female powers. I like to use some old and
even worn-looking materials mixed with the new. In this piece,
the black net dress with the white beading brings a fragile
element and many of the buttons are old.

Therese May
San Jose, California
Rose
Various fabrics and acrylic paint. Machine appliquéd. 66″ x 56″

"Rose"—a symbol of gratitude, love, appreciation, peace and grace.

Terrie H. Mangat
Cincinnati, Ohio
Shrine to the Beginning
Cotton and painted canvas, assorted trinkets and toys, ceramic
vase with found objects, electric lights and metallic cut "zinnias."
Painted, pieced, embroidered and appliquéd using both direct
and reverse appliqué. Quilted by Sue Rule. 98″ x 104″, photo-
graphed against a white background.

This quilt is a documentation of my progress from a very
conservative beginning as a quiltmaker and artist to a state of
freedom in expression. It also commemorates the beginning of
my marriage and life as an independent adult.

Nancy Crow
Baltimore, Ohio
Mexican Wheels I
Cottons and blends. Machine pieced by the artist and hand quilted by Rose Augenstein. 82″ x 82″

"Mexican Wheels I" is so titled because this quilt is based on the "sense of gaiety" I perceive in the Mexican culture, in Mexican folk art, in the incredible use of color that is pervasive throughout all of Mexico. It is an outgrowth of seeing oxcart wheels painted in graphic designs and of viewing and trying to absorb the wealth of detail in Mexican churches. And it is based on the floral blouses worn by the Indian women in Oaxaca. The black and white fabrics imitate lace and crochet around the neck-openings of these blouses. But the black and white fabrics also act as a form of a drawing.

Ann Adams
San Antonio, Texas
Polyfest
Cotton, hand dyed with Procion dye. Machine pieced, hand appliquéd, some fabrics heat fused to base, machine quilted. 43" x 43"

I enjoy questioning the idea of what a quilt should look like. I wanted to challenge people's assumptions of what is considered beautiful so I used materials most people would consider ugly. In my search for more spontaneity in design, I found fusing fabric a good alternative. I have an on-going interest in surface pattern design on fabric and have become fond of the wealth of design material found in the loud polyester neckties of the last decades.

Patricia Malarcher
Englewood, New Jersey
Detour
Mixed media, including mylar, linen, canvas, acrylic paint and vinyl. Machine sewn and painted. 51" x 51"

"Detour" is an experimental piece that evolved from playing with variations in the components of a modular unit. It was an attempt to free myself from my usual pristine surfaces and formal compositions in order to see what possibilities lay beyond them. The title was suggested by the prevalence of a bright orange that reminded me of road construction apparatus, and also by the work's look of unfinished rawness. "Detour" also refers to the fact that the piece deviated from my established direction for the purpose of renewal.

Uta Büchel and **Ellen Harlizius-Klück**
Neuss, West Germany
Weather-beaten Roof
Silk, hand-painted by Ellen Harlizius-Klück. Hand pieced and hand quilted by Uta Büchel. 50″ x 41″

This quilt is the result of a series of photos which I made. When I could not find appropriate commercial fabrics with which to execute my idea, I asked Ellen to help me dye silk. She offered to paint each individual "roof-tile" in order to get a three-dimensional impression. The painting allowed her to produce effects on the silk similar to those weather would have caused on roofing tiles.

Deborah Felix
San Diego, California
Fishing for the Intangible
Canvas, fabric and paint. Hand stamped, appliquéd and sewn by
the artist and quilted by Lynn Kough. 100″ x 69″

"Fishing for the Intangible" is like a vast ocean filled with
piranhas that lurk behind sharp coral reefs.

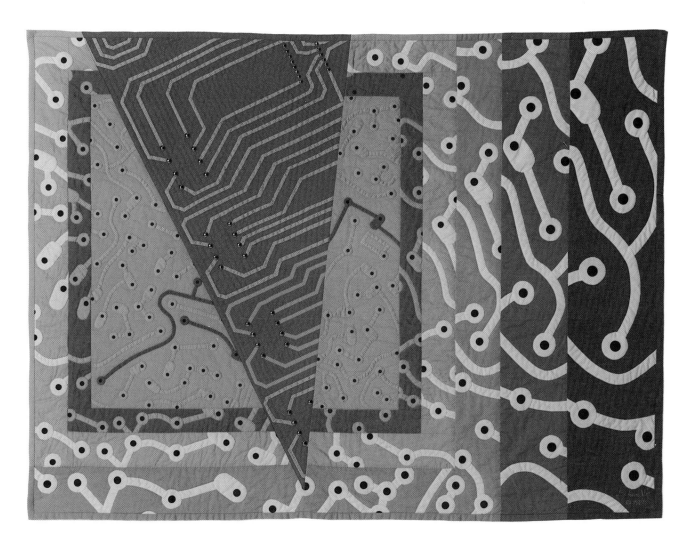

Robin Schwalb
New York, New York
PCB Bop
Cottons, hand-stenciled fabric, metal studs. Machine and hand pieced, hand appliquéd and hand quilted. 55″ x 41″

The initial inspiration for this quilt was both sublime and ridiculous—a combination of an Edward Weston photograph ("Sandstone Erosion, Point Lobos," 1942) and the sweat stains on Joe Cocker's brocade shirt during a rousing 1987 performance. It evolved into the lovely patterns of PCBs—printed circuit boards. While I hesitate to hang a lot of heavy ideological baggage onto what is essentially a lyrical, happy piece, the viewer is encouraged to maintain a thoughtful attitude towards technological innovation.

AWARD OF EXCELLENCE

Ardyth Davis
Leesburg, Virginia
Horizon I/Blue
Silk. Hand painted, creased, punctured and stitched. 68″ x 70″

I am continuing to explore color gradation washes in painting fabric, in addition to treating the surface in different ways to create texture. The "Horizon" series developed from pastel studies of the Maine coast. After brushing dyes on the silk, I then pleat and gather it before employing a steaming process which sets both the creases and the dyes.

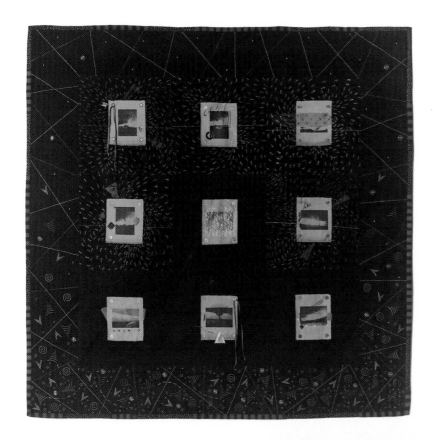

Merrill Mason
Jersey City, New Jersey
Tornado I
Cotton and blended fabrics, color Xeroxed images, textile pigments, metallic thread, buttons, beads, found objects. Stamped with hand-carved rubber stamps, machine pieced and embroidered, hand embellished. 49″ x 49″

This is the first in a series of quilts using the tornado as a metaphor for physical and emotional turmoil. For three years I lived out of boxes while renovating an old house. I wanted to express that turbulence, but as the quilt progressed, other more distant times of purely emotional turmoil began to surface, along with the humor it took to cope with those difficult times.

Judith Larzelere
Dedham, Massachusetts
Chains of Blood, Tears of Rust
Cotton fabrics and polyester fleece batting. Machine pieced and quilted. 98″ x 87″

My heart goes out to all victims of torture and political imprisonment. This quilt is made in their honor.

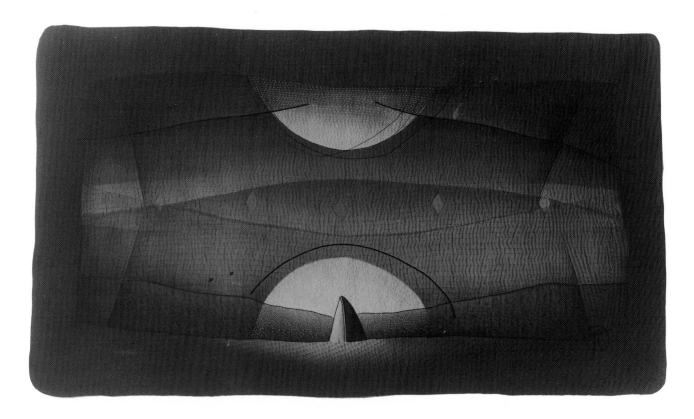

Jan Irvine
New South Wales, Australia
Elipse II
Silk fabric and wool batting. Airbrush dyed and handstitched.
79" x 44"

The visual elements of my work explore the qualities of light and
visual movement within a context, usually landscape. My imagery
has personal meaning but the viewer is free to respond directly
without need for interpretation. Technically, I draw from the
traditions of quilting and embroidery but use the stitch for its
design components of embossing and marking the surface. I
enjoy a fully stitched surface for the drape-like quality of the
finished work and the charm of the stitch itself.

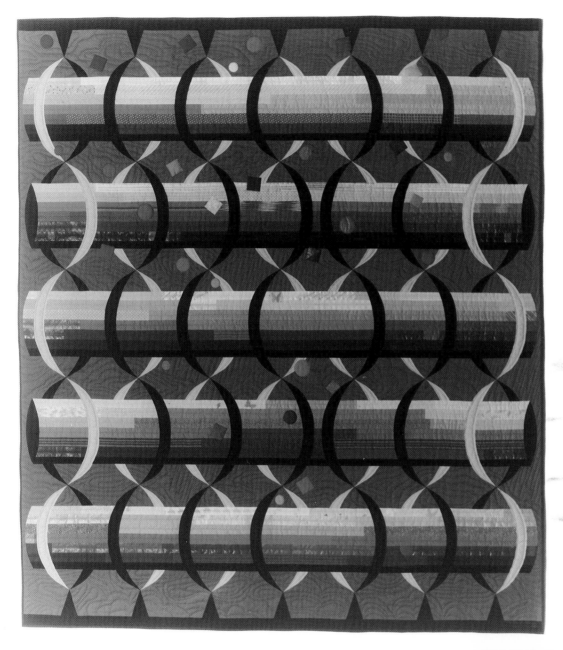

Liesel Niesner
Osnabrük, West Germany
"...ein Regenbogen für GREENPEACE."
Cotton fabrics. Machine pieced, hand appliquéd and hand
quilted. 69″ x 79″

I enjoy creating a three-dimensional work out of such a flat
medium as fabric and delight in playing with colors and shadows.
This work is dedicated to the organization Greenpeace, for
struggling to keep the beauty of the earth for our children.

**DOMINI McCARTHY AWARD FOR
EXCEPTIONAL CRAFTSMANSHIP**

detail

Nancy Halpern
Natick, Massachusetts
Anemone Rag
Commercial and hand-dyed fabrics. Cyanotype printing, hand pieced and hand quilted. 73″ x 71″

This is a bi-coastal four-poster futon quilt started at Point Bonita, California, and finished at Deer Isle, Maine. Constructed from fabrics begged from quiltmakers coast to coast, it was stitched on planes and in airports. This quilt somehow gives a Japanese slant to a straightforward New England shape.

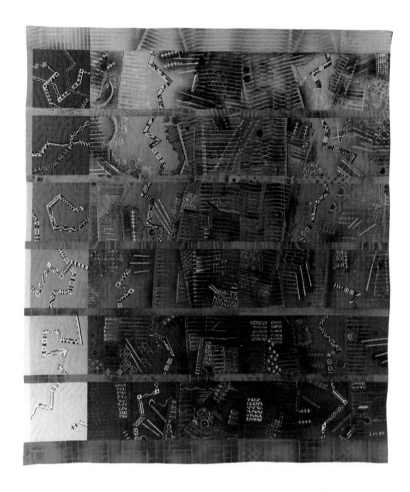

Linda MacDonald
Willits, California
Weaving Zebra Dancers
Cotton fabric and batting. Air-brushed, hand
painted and hand quilted. 47" x 55"
Collection of Peter Brooks.

I have been air brushing with various stencils,
sticks, toys and grids. Then I use brush painting
to bring out images, patterns and spatial relationships that I see. I have been reacquainting myself
with bold patterning more indigenous to primal
cultures.

Katherine Knauer
New York, New York
Planet X Comix
Cotton fabrics. Airbrushed, using stencils hand-
cut by the artist; pieced and hand quilted.
87" x 84"

The imagery here is deliberately enigmatic so
that each viewer must construct his or her own
fantasy of the actions depicted.

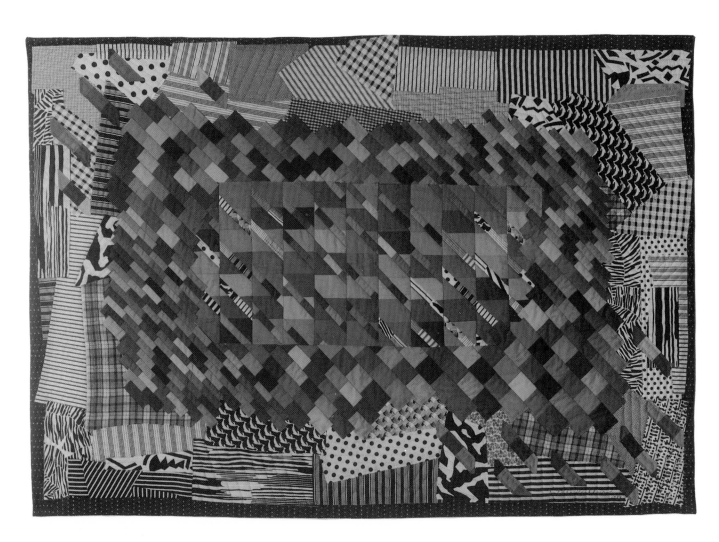

Esther Parkhurst
Los Angeles, California
Black & White with Raw Edges
Domestic and imported cottons. Machine and hand pieced,
machine and hand quilted. 59″ x 41″

After making the central area using color and a precise machine-
stitched construction, I felt the need to contrast this with the
arbitrary shapes, leaving the raw edges exposed. I continued the
contrast formula by machine quilting the central area in the ditch,
and hand quilting the outer area in an arbitrary pattern.

Ursula Gerber-Senger
Männedorf, Switzerland
Polarity
Kork-skin and raw silk, hand spun and hand woven. Hand pieced and quilted. 72″ x 57″

"Polarity"—back to nature, in which simple forms add up to complex structures, one clay-colored in its full variation of brightness and—on the top and in the centers of gravity—others that are blue and red, creating simultaneous contrast and tension. The work interprets polarity through a regular circular geometric macro-structure (handwoven, hand sewn), coupled with a very diversified natural micro-structure (raw silk). The tension and contrast created stand for the variety and sensitivity of nature—the genesis and causality of polarity—the basic requirement of life.

Linda Levin
Wayland, Massachusetts
Pallone: Siena Di Mattina
Cotton fabrics dyed with fiber reactive dyes. Machine pieced. 82″ x 52″

This piece is one of a series based on four flights over Siena, Italy, in a hot air balloon. The aerial views were exhilarating and have provided me with a rich stock of memories to draw upon.

Roxana Bartlett
Boulder, Colorado
Wild Snow Chase
Broadcloth, flannel and satin, treated with dye, fabric paint and printer's ink. Pieced, appliquéd and quilted by hand. 59″ x 59″

The landscapes of my quilts are not real but transformed by emotion into ones distilled and evocative as in a dream or a memory of long ago. My ideas are stimulated by the changing seasons and the hours of the day with their inevitable symbolism of the passage of time and lives, and also by the spirit of myths wherein each animal, tree and mountain of the landscape has a power and meaning beyond its immediate identity.

Joy Saville
Princeton, New Jersey
Dance of Chi
Cotton, silk, linen, wool/voile interlining, muslin backing.
Pieced, stitched and mounted on a hidden frame. 65″ x 44″

My work is informed by color. Color expresses concepts and feelings. During the process of manipulation there is a time when color speaks for itself. I listen. When I hear it, I am transformed.

Photo provided by artist.

Terrie H. Mangat
Cincinnati, Ohio
Sky Stones
Cottons and blends, extruded acrylic paint, beads. Pieced, embroidered and appliquéd using both direct and reverse appliqué. Quilted by Sue Rule. 88″ x 98″

This quilt was inspired by a fireworks display which was exploded over Lake Michigan in the summer. The stones on the beach have been thrust into the air with the energy of a blast. It represents celebration of friendship and richness of life.

Darcy Usilton
Madison, Wisconsin
Putting the Guise to Bed
Satin, velvet, yarn, metallic and embroidery threads. Appliquéd
crazy quilt. 37″ x 53″

Guise—garb, dress, hence semblance. Women and men—fantasy
thoughts while painting the living room ended up with me
thinking "Let's put the 'guise' to bed."

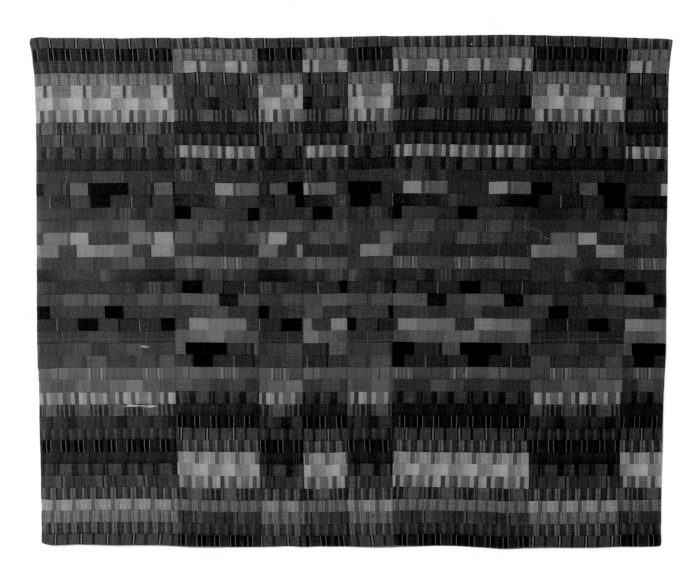

Emily Zopf
Seattle, Washington
Water Music
Cotton and blended fabrics, cotton batting. Machine pieced and
hand quilted. 78″ x 61

I have found that cutting plaid fabrics into narrow strips and
reassembling them creates interesting rhythms. The rhythms
change with the spacing of the stripes of color and the
juxtaposition of other fabrics. In this quilt I see the patterns of
rippling water and the joyful colors of Handel's "Water Music."

Robin Schwalb
New York, New York
Rosetta Stone
Cottons and blends, some hand painted. Machine pieced, hand appliquéd and hand quilted. 40″ x 71″

The "Rosetta Stone," an ancient stela with a bilingual inscription in three 'alphabets,' provided the key to deciphering ancient Egyptian hieroglyphs. This fact gives it monumentality far beyond its modest size. My quilted homage substitutes medieval, industrial and post-industrial technological symbols and languages for the Greek and Egyptian of the original Stone. There are alchemical references hidden in the quilting in the borders. Despite the 20th century's explosive increase in scientific and technological knowledge, many questions remain. When faced with a particularly sanctimonious pronouncement about the latest discovery, it amuses me to think that once upon a time, alchemy was at the cutting edge of science.

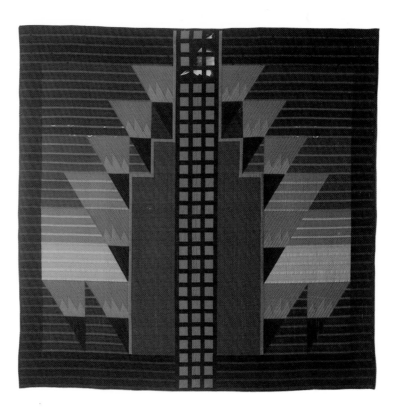

Jeanne Martin
Seattle, Washington
Untitled
Cotton fabric and polyester batting. Machine pieced and hand quilted. 81″ x 80″

This quilt is one of several I made which are based on architectural images. In these quilts I was interested in representing, in a general way, human structures in a natural setting.

Holley Junker
Sacramento, California
Q'est Seurat? Seurat!
Pinked circles of cotton fabrics. Layered to blend colors and
create images, machine stitched to top, hand tied. 59″ x 42″
Collection of Silvia and Erwin Potts.

At the back of my fantasy forest is a meadow filled with ever-
blooming wildflowers. It is a safe and happy place.

Elizabeth A. Busch
Bangor, Maine
Child Dream
Acrylic paint on raw 7 oz. canvas, colored pencils and chalk, photocopy transfer, beads, embroidery floss, commercial fabric, cotton batting and a painted antique pressed back chair. Machine pieced and appliquéd, hand quilted. 67″ x 72″ x 36″ deep, photographed against a white background.

The mummy of Nes-Min, Priest of Akhim, is wrapped in strips of cloth, preserved in physical form for his afterlife. Seeing his carefully wrapped body inspired a series of bed quilts about the bed. We spend at least one-third of our lives under fabric in bed. It is a time and space of comfort and warmth, joy, love, fear, sorrow, sleep, departure and dreams. "Child Dream" is about that time in childhood. The chair is the presence of the person being called to take the child out of the nightmare, but alas, her presence is in another realm, and the joy of a new day/dream is only peripheral.

Glenda King
Lexington, Kentucky
LCC 2:3
Cottons and blends. Machine pieced and hand
quilted, embroidered signature. 58″ x 58″

"LCC 2:3" is an exploration of the complex
variations possible with log cabin construction
techniques when developed along non-traditional lines. Subtitled "Structural Conundrum," this
quilt reflects my ongoing fascination with mazes,
optical illusions and bold geometric designs.

Judy Becker
Newton, Massachusetts
African Rhythms
Cotton and rayon challis. Machine pieced and
hand quilted. 55″ x 59″

When I quilt in the late afternoon, I often listen to
jazz on the radio. The Modern Jazz Quartet series,
of which "African Rhythms" is number four,
started with a linear design of a stylized number
"4" in the repeating blocks. But as the work
evolved it took on a rhythm of its own, as
improvisational as a jam session.

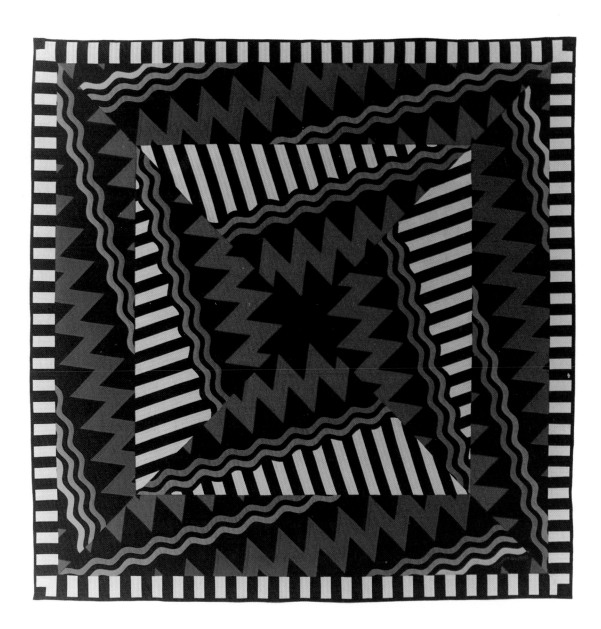

Jane A. Sassaman
Chicago, Illinois
Zig-Zag Spiral
Cotton fabrics and batting. Machine pieced, hand appliquéd and
machine quilted. 50″ x 50″
Collection of Tom Hennessey.

"Zig-Zag" is the fifth in a series of spiral quilts. Spirals symbolize
the cycles of life and the centers from which they radiate (the self,
nature, etc.). Spirals, plus some great spring thunderstorms,
provided the inspiration for this piece.

Teresa Cooper Jacobs
Seattle, Washington
Through the Hourglass (or Big Bo Peep)
Cotton and blended fabrics, Procion dyes and Eurotex fabric
paint, cotton batting. Batiked, hand painted, hand appliquéd,
machine pieced and machine quilted. 26″ x 24″

This quilt and a variation of the traditional "Little Bo Peep"
nursery rhyme grew out of each other as I explored images of
aging. They tell about the struggle to "let go" as one encounters
losses of one kind or another. The quilted figure especially
portrays my vision of myself (as a much older woman who has
learned to "let go" and is experiencing fullness of life). I
experimented with figure development using dyes, paint and
piecing, along with machine stitching, as integral parts of the
design.

Photo provided by artist.

Inge Hueber
Köln, West Germany
Diabolo
Hand-dyed cotton. Machine pieced and hand quilted. 75″ x 65″

In "Diabolo" I tried to mix different formal elements: irregular patchwork and regular stripes, straight and curved lines, busy and calm colors. In blending these contrasts, I believe each part should gain something from the others. In working with my self-dyed fabric I try to go on and stretch the possibilities of this special material.

Cynthia Lambert and **Janet Lorini**
Pittsburgh, Pennsylvania
St. Irving and the Archangels
Silk, beads, Procion dyes and textile paint and found objects. Embroidered and quilted by hand and machine. 99″ x 52″

This work represents the joyful effort of two artists with distinctly different styles. St. Irving is an imaginary creature who flies around Pittsburgh sprinkling good fortune on hard-working, talented and humble artists.

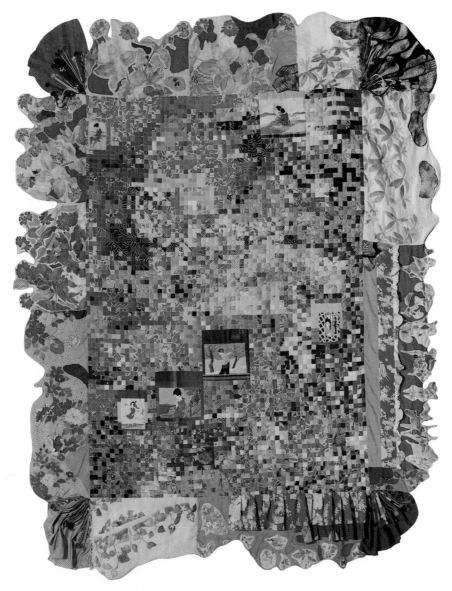

detail

Ikuko Fujishiro
Funabashi-shi, Japan
A Burning Heart
Fabric and ties from antique silk Japanese kimonos. Hand pieced,
appliquéd and painted. 77″ x 98″

I wanted to express "a woman's heart" by colors. It is sincere and
burning. A heart should be calm and sensitive. I would like to
make my heart like that.

Judi Warren
Maumee, Ohio
March 28, 1986: Rain at Fushimi Inari
Cotton, lamé, hand-painted and hand-printed cottons, silver and
iridescent beads. Machine pieced/strip pieced, hand quilted,
appliquéd and embroidered. 88″ x 72″

On March 28, 1986 it rained in Kyoto. "Rain at Fushimi Inari" is a
memory....of paper cranes, wooden prayer tablets, paper fortunes
tied in the trees, of new leaves and old torii gates washed in misty
raindrops and soft light that made already-spectacular colors even
more intense. Because this quilt is about a place I cannot forget,
one paper fortune is embroidered with the words NIHON NI
MATA KAERITAI (Return again to Japan.)

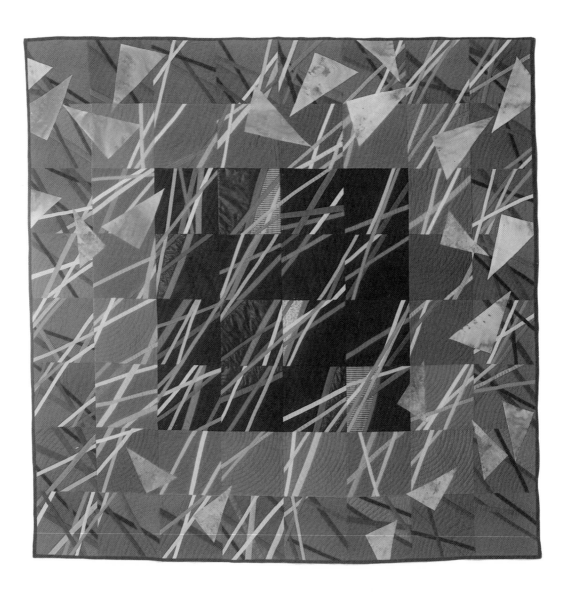

Sue Alvarez
Fries, Virginia
That's the Way It Goes...
Commercial cottons, hand-dyed fabric and ribbon. Machine pieced, appliquéd by hand and machine, machine quilted. 62″ x 62″

This quilt was inspired by a song I heard in the summer of 1986. I am not outwardly musical so the production of this quilt was my way of sharing the silent music in my heart. My work is totally important to me. I think about making art all the time and I am inspired by everything around me.

Elizabeth A. Busch
Bangor, Maine
When We Were Young
Acrylic paint on raw 7 oz. cotton canvas, colored pencils, Procion dyes, commercial fabric and cotton batting. Hand brushed and air brushed, machine pieced, hand appliquéd and hand quilted. 68″ x 80″

This is one of a series of bed quilts *about* the bed. "When We Were Young" is about that time in early marriage when children are infants and all dreams are sweet and full of hope and love.

BEST OF SHOW AWARD

Ann Joyce
Columbus, Ohio
Ex Libris
Cottons, blends and "decorator" fabric. Machine pieced, hand
and machine quilted. 42" x 28

"Ex Libris" is simply a tribute to books and my love of public and
private libraries. There are "still lifes" of books within the piece. I
wanted to endow the books with magical qualities by embellish-
ing the "covers" with richly-patterned fabrics. For me, though, the
real magic of books begins once the cover is lifted and one enters
any number of exotic worlds.

Miriam Nathan Roberts
Berkeley, California
The Museum
Cottons and blends. Machine pieced and hand appliquéd by the artist. Hand quilted by Sarah Hershberger. 58″ x 63″

"The Museum" was designed not long after a visit to the New Museum of Contemporary Art in Los Angeles. The quilt depicts people coming to the museum to visit the various galleries of contemporary art. If you look closely you will see the ticket taker, sitting with his telephone, awaiting your arrival.

Miriam Nathan Roberts
Berkeley, California
Letting Go
Hand-dyed and hand-painted cotton fabric. Machine pieced by the artist and hand quilted by Sarah Hershberger. 69″ x 69″

This is the sixth quilt in an interweave series. The other five are tightly controlled, all lines straight and taut. Having worked within that self-imposed discipline, I felt the need to rebel, to let go.

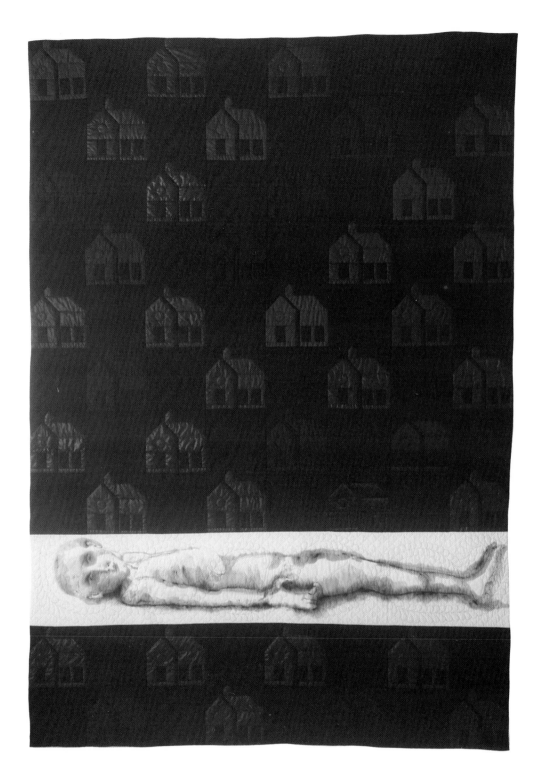

Cherry Partee
Edmonds, Washington
The Epiphany of Joanna Burden
Cotton and acetate fabrics, polyester fiber-fil batting. Machine pieced, hand painted with Deka fiber paint, hand quilted. 70″ x 102″

I began this piece thinking about race relations, My Lai, and the guilt we all must bear simply because we are members of the human race. We are what we exemplify of our past, and that collective and personal past can so bind us that our scope for individual action seems very small. As Americans, we have striven to break the rudder of history; even, as women, we try to recover it. Without that historical and cultural consciousness we are condemned to drift into an unchosen, memory-less future.

Jan Myers-Newbury
Pittsburgh, Pennsylvania
Night Swarm
100 percent cotton muslin, dyed and tie-dyed with Procion dyes. Machine pieced and machine quilted. 38" x 34"
From a private collection.

"Night Swarm" is part of a movement toward more "expression" in my work. While formal design concerns are still important to me, "prettiness" is less so. Working with tie-dyed fabrics has moved me away from total control and calculation into a realm in which I am much less self-assured, that of partial chaos. I find myself responding on an emotional level.

Carol H. Gersen
Boonsboro, Maryland
Chinese Coins Variation: Skylines
Commercial and hand-dyed cotton fabrics. Machine pieced and hand quilted. 56" x 56"

"Chinese Coins" is the name of a traditional Amish pattern based on the abacus. I arranged the usual rows of "Chinese Coins" into a grid, which was then placed on a graded background of my own hand-dyed cottons. I continue to enjoy this pattern because it provides a format for joyful work with color.

Helen Giddens
Mesquite, Texas
Armadillo Highway
Cottons and blends. Machine pieced, hand appliquéd and hand
quilted. 70″ x 82″

When I moved from Oklahoma to Texas I noticed several
armadillos (dead and alive) all along the interstate highway. I
suppose I could call it a "Road To" quilt.

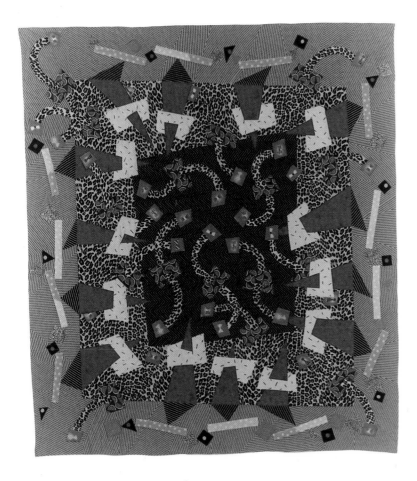

Ellen Oppenheimer
Oakland, California
New Year's Eve Party
Commercial and overdyed fabrics. Machine pieced, machine and hand quilted. 76″ x 84″

I started working on this quilt toward the end of 1986; I was thinking of friends who were celebrating the New Year by going out dancing and partying. My plans were to stay home and go to sleep early, which made me feel like a dull person who never did anything exciting and risky. This quilt was my risk taking excitement, with wildly dancing forms in the center on a dance floor, tables around the dance floor with champagne (the pink fabric with the black lines made me think of champagne) and then barricades around the outside with people waiting to get in. Everyone is having so much fun that they are dancing all over the place. Things are at strange angles as if we have had too much to drink.

Ann Kowaleski
Mt. Pleasant, Michigan
Masked Oaxacan Stilt Dancers
Wool, lamé, handwoven Guatemalan fabric, silk, cotton, cotton blends, African batik and satin, braiding, mylar, sequins and buttons. Embroidered, appliquéd and pieced by the artist, quilted by Katie Mast. 75″ x 51″

Since 1984 I have been working on a series of dancing and performing quilts. I am influenced by the people and events in my everyday life, as well as my travels. Many times the events are real. This work is my response to festivals and celebrations of deeply held cultural beliefs that prevail in parts of rural Mexico. The central female figure represents the lead dancer, the Mother Earth figure. Many Mexican Indians still live very close to nature. Mask makers are disappearing and this is my attempt to exalt them.

Cherry Partee
Edmonds, Washington
Long Distance Call
Cotton fabrics, Cotton Classic batting. Machine appliquéd and
machine quilted. 78″ x 72″

This piece is about the desire for closeness and intimacy, about
wanting and not knowing what is wanted.

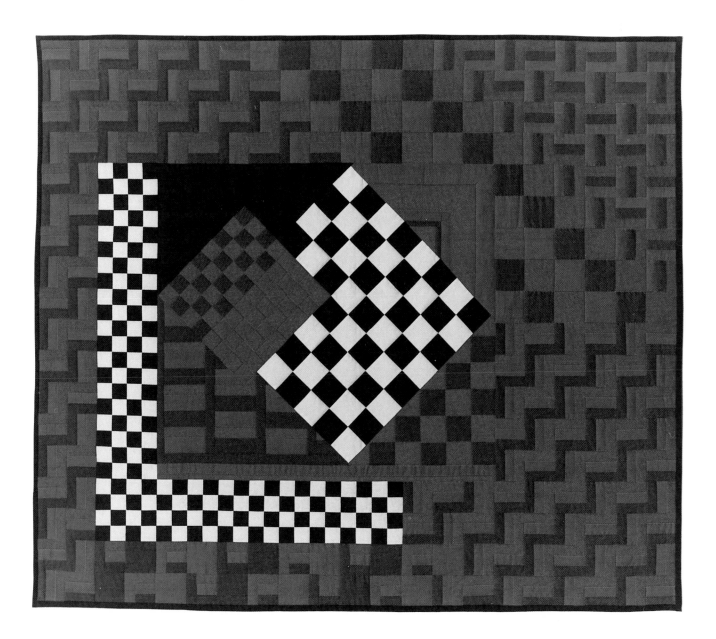

Suma Smith
Kingwood, Texas
Primary Fantasy
Cotton fabric and polyester batting. Machine pieced and hand
quilted in the seams of the design. 63" x 54"

One of the main focuses of my work is combining traditional
design elements in innovative configurations. I particularly enjoy
challenging my imagination by placing limitations of one sort or
another on a given work. In this piece the challenge was to create
work predominantly from "Rail Fence" blocks.

Rebecca Speakes
Minneapolis, Minnesota
HeatWave
Cotton-blended chintz and tricot lamé. Machine
pieced and hand quilted. 44″ x 44″

Summer in the city—everywhere shimmering
heat rises from pavement. The blurring relentless
sun bakes the earth. Blinding heat leaves after-
images of snowcaps and glaciers breaking into
the sea.

Patty Hawkins
Lyons, Colorado
Cactus People
Cotton and blended fabrics, oilcloth, plastic,
buttons, string, yarn, raffia. Machine appliquéd
and machine quilted. 76″ x 92″

"Cactus People" resulted from taking the subtle
Southwest colors and adding the surprise
element. Drunkard's Path is a favorite foil for
bouncing off the design composition, which
adds depth, further created by the quiltline of
faraway vistas. The desert appears so barren with
no excitement. Upon closer scrutiny, who's to
say the local vegetation isn't really enjoying the
good life? No crows or traffic jams mar life for
these happy Cactus People, i.e., Organ Pipe
cactus, Bishop's Cap cactus, Crown cactus, Bunny
Ears cactus, Crown of Thorns cactus and Easter
Lily cactus.

Clare M. Murray
Canton, Ohio
Travelog #1: Aldstadt
Cotton fabric and polyester batting. Hand painted with Procion
fiber reactive dyes, hand quilted. 52" x 59"

"Travelog #1" is based on a design I had drawn while travelling in
Europe in 1987. It was very much influenced by the art works of
the cubist period that I saw in the many galleries and museums I
visited. At the same time, I had a chance to create some quilts that
were more architectural in nature and that also incorporated
areas of transparency. Initially I decided to paint this work as a
study for other pieces I intended to make. By painting the design
on fabric and then quilting the painting, I was able to work out the
technical aspects of piecing the unusual angles presented in the
design—something I have been able to carry out in the other
pieces in the series.

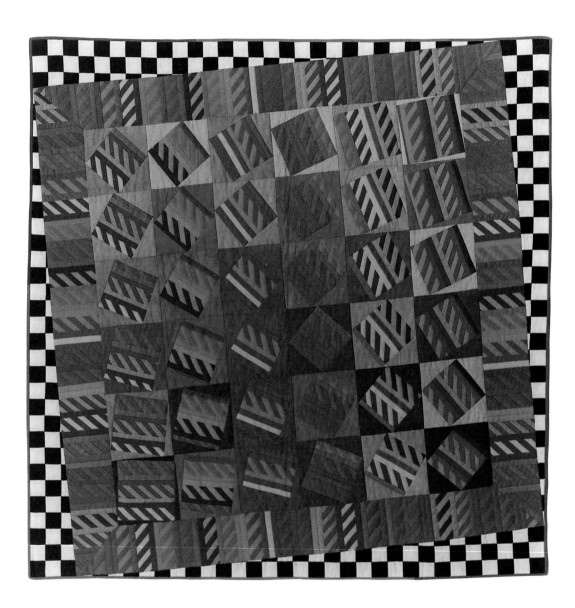

Chris Wolf Edmonds
Lawrence, Kansas
Left-Handed Compliments
Hand-dyed and commercially-dyed cotton fabric. Machine pieced
and quilted, hand appliquéd on back. 50″ x 50″

I continue to be intrigued by the illusion of light, depth and
motion in the two-dimensional quilt surface through the
manipulation of value, color and design.

INVITATIONAL WORK:
Quilt National '89 Juror

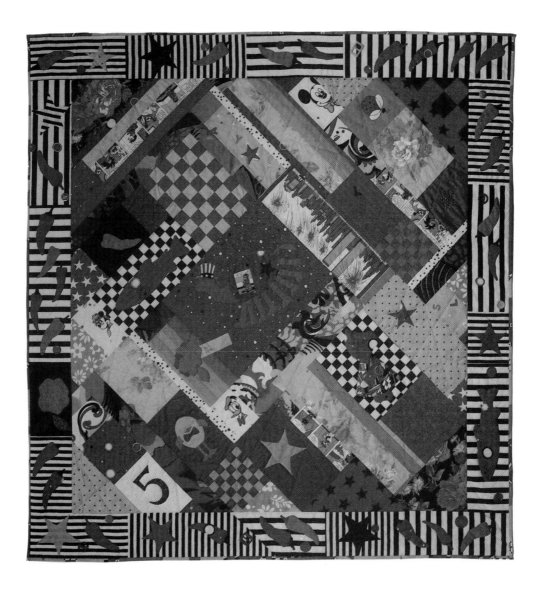

Yvonne Porcella
Modesto, California
Riding an 8 Legged Camel
Cotton fabrics, buttons. Machine pieced, hand appliquéd and
hand quilted. 64″ x 67″
From the collection of the High Museum of Art, Atlanta, Georgia.
Gift of Martha and Pat Connell and purchased with funds from the
Decorative Arts Acquisition Trust.

At Christmas a few years ago, I received a battery operated camel
which uses eight legs to walk. Since then we've had races to see if
the camel is faster than the wind-up walking chicken. The quilt
was done as a remembrance of these happy times and of my
collection of plastic flowers, decorations and toys. In keeping
with this playful theme, I've included familiar American images.

INVITATIONAL WORK:
Quilt National '89 Juror

Janet Page-Kessler
New York, New York
Still Life V/VI
Cottons and blends with some fabrics over-painted. Machine
appliquéd, machine embroidered, machine quilted. 52″ x 22″

This series began with still life drawings and a design problem of
"surrounding patterns." Color is one of my primary concerns, as
are space, texture, shape and value. I have enjoyed the challenge
of manipulating the commercial fabrics to make them work
within the context of the piece. Working in this collage format
offers a wonderful sense of freedom of expression which differs
from that offered by the grid format of traditional quiltmaking.

Patsy Allen
Greensboro, North Carolina
Deco Pinwheel VI: Threshold
Cotton fabrics, some silk-screened by hand. Machine pieced, appliquéd and quilted. 56" x 56"

This quilt is part of a series of square "pinwheel" quilts using an Art Deco theme. While keeping the same basic design structure, each quilt is an exploration of color relationships and patterning. As the series grew, the quilts acquired asymmetrical borders and dark "barrier" lines. In "Threshold" the barrier lines serve as the demarcation of the entrance to the quilt.

Joyce Marquess Carey
Madison, Wisconsin
Glad Rags
Satin, lamé, velveteen and corduroy. Machine pieced. Each piece measures approximately 32" x 54".
Three separate pieces are photographed against a black background.

"Glad Rags" have a life of their own. These cheerful little flags remind us of the happy fabrics in our lives—bright scarves, pennants, streamers, towels popping on a windy clothesline.

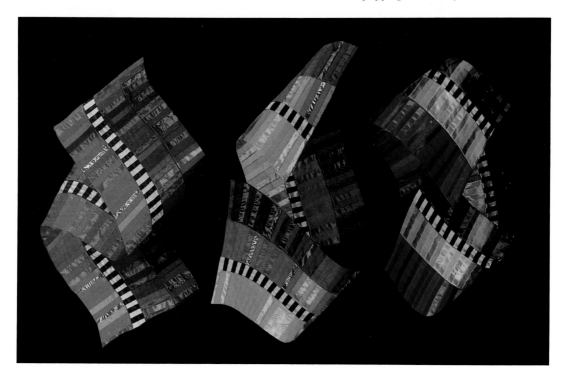

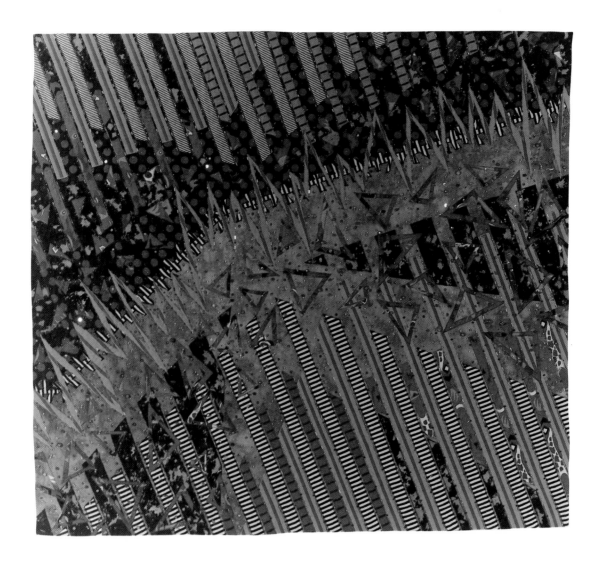

David Walker
Cincinnati, Ohio
Renascence for Rebecca
Cottons and blends, control-bleached and dyed fabrics, beads, sequins and fabric paint. Machine pieced and appliquéd. 61″ x 55″

"The soul can split the sky in two and let the face of God shine through." In her poem "Renascence," Edna St. Vincent Millay celebrates the power of the human spirit to renew itself and to create life from seemingly desperate and hopeless circumstances. She speaks of taking charge and of reasserting control over her own life, and, in the process, she is able to identify herself with the immensity of the universe and the unity of God. "I breathed my soul back into me"—this is Miss Millay's confident anthem of courage as well as her determined affirmation of life.

From Quilt National's Coordinator

Quilt National '89, the sixth of the Dairy Barn's international competitions, marks the start of the exhibition's second decade. As I think about the works in this collection, I find myself recalling my impressions of the first Quilt National and considering how involvement with Quilt National has changed and enriched my life.

My first visit to Quilt National '79 (and there were many since I live only ten minutes from the Dairy Barn) was indescribably exciting. Although I had been interested in many different kinds of needlework, functional quilts never held much appeal for me. After seeing the '79 exhibit I realized that quilts didn't have to be made for beds. I was fascinated by the individual interpretations of traditional design elements and ways in which the artists had utilized techniques and materials long associated with quilt-making.

Two years later I served as a member of the Quilt National steering committee and found it difficult to believe how much work went into the organization and presentation of a Quilt National. An unexpected opportunity to take a workshop in design development and frequent visits to the exhibit gave me the desire (and courage) to create my own original quilt.

In late 1982, I had been asked to help process the entries for Quilt National '83. The next thing I knew I was hired as Quilt National's coordinator. I soon came to regard every quilt and its maker as personal friends. In studying the entries I noticed changes in quilts by artists who had been in earlier shows, and I was enthralled by the creativity of those whose work was new to me. At the same time I discovered that among the traditional quilts I had so readily dismissed years earlier there were, indeed, many examples of innovation and originality.

My involvement with the '85, '87 and '89 Quilt Nationals has given me the privilege of studying every entry and identifying elements which create works that excite both wonder and admiration in the viewer. And it has been a special pleasure to see more and more artists the world over choosing the quilt medium to express their visions and ideas.

Quilt National has had a profound influence on my life. There isn't a day that goes by without my being involved in some way with quilts: they now adorn the walls of my home; I treasure the friendship of countless quilt artists from all over the world; and the administration of Quilt National continues to provide me with challenges and great satisfaction.

The last ten years have been very special, and I look forward to seeing the course Quilt National will take in the 1990's.

Hilary M. Fletcher
Coordinator

Quilt National '81 Installation.   Quilt National '79 Installation.

The Dairy Barn Southeastern Ohio Cultural Arts Center, Athens, Ohio.

Quilt National '87 Installation at the American Craft Museum
Photo by Taylor Dabney.

Quilt National '83 Installation.

Quilt National '89 Touring Exhibition

A collection of approximately 50 works from Quilt National '89 will be on display in galleries and institutions throughout the United States and Japan. The tour will begin in August 1989 and continue through December 1991. Included on the itinerary are the following:

8/1/89-9/30/89: St. Louis, Missouri - St. Louis Centre (Benefit exhibit for the Women's Self Help Center)

11/26/89-1/5/90: Anchorage, Alaska - Anchorage Museum of History and Art

1/10/90-6/30/90: Japan - Selected cities and venues

11/1/90-12/31/90: Lowell, Massachusetts - New England Quilt Museum

The Quilt National '89 Touring Exhibition is produced and managed by The Dairy Barn Southeastern Ohio Cultural Arts Center in Athens, Ohio.

About the Dairy Barn

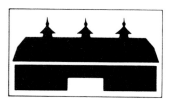

The Dairy Barn Southeastern Ohio Cultural Arts Center is recognized widely for the high quality, unique programming that has been created by its professional staff and dedicated volunteers.

Quilt National joins such other events as American Contemporary Works in Wood, BasketWeave and the National Jigsaw Puzzle Championships and Design Exhibition on the Dairy Barn's diverse calendar of events. Fine arts exhibitions, performances and arts and crafts festivals add to the many uses for the 75-year-old structure.

Listed on the National Register of Historic Places, the Dairy Barn is an architectural gem with more than 7,000 square feet of exhibition space. The gently rolling Appalachian foothills provide a rare setting for this special facility.

Prior to the 1988 season, the Dairy Barn underwent extensive renovation, and it now can be used on a year-round basis for both its own programs and special events sponsored by numerous community and regional organizations.

Through its six Quilt National exhibitions and their accompanying publications, the Dairy Barn has played a major role in showcasing and promoting the contemporary quilt as a lively and challenging art form.

Quilt National '83 Installation at Miami University Art Museum.
Photo provided by Miami University.

A Look Back

Quilt National
- A Look Back

When it began in 1979, Quilt National was the first and only juried exhibit dedicated to providing a showcase for those artists whose work deviated from the traditional definitions of "quilt." Changes in the concept of "quilt" were initially rather subtle, but as the decade passed, new and exciting trends appeared and continued to develop. It seems appropriate that, as we approach the brink of a new decade, we take time to look back at Quilt National's history.

Visitors to the first Quilt National were astonished by the maze of texture, shape and color. Most of the pieces were like traditional quilts in that they were "fabric sandwiches" bound together by hand stitching, but their sizes and shapes indicated that they were not intended for beds. These works of art were intended for walls. Only this type of display would allow the viewer to see them from the distance necessary for the images to be fully appreciated. While many of the works displayed an obvious relationship to traditional design elements, others were very personal statements utilizing unexpected color combinations and new arrangements of shapes.

Quilt National '81 included more quilts made for walls, but also had some made for ceilings—Virginia Jacobs's trio of quilted kites, complete with long tails. Fewer of the quilts than in the earlier show were made from commercial cottons. An increasing number of quiltmakers were dyeing their own fabrics in order to achieve the very subtle color variations that were unavailable with commercial fabrics. Works in the '81 exhibit included cyanotyped, batiked, silkscreened, air-brushed, painted, ink-drawn, rubber-stamped and color-Xeroxed images, ribbons and paper. A few artists were even using machine quilting and other techniques which had not been previously utilized. At the same time, however, other artists were electing to do much of their work by hand and had honed their skills to create masterpieces whose technical characteristics were above reproach.

Those who visited Quilt National '83 saw a quilted flying carpet, complete with battery pack and twinkling lights. They saw a beautiful hand-painted dragon on the lining of a multi-colored quilted kimono, and they saw a collection of handmade hats floating above a fantasy lake. The quilts not only included almost every imaginable kind of fabric but were embellished with everything from elaborate embroidery to fishing hooks, rubber worms and golden rings.

Although there had always been international involvement in Quilt National, the works in the '85 exhibit represented six countries other than the United States. The artists continued to explore the possibilities provided by the newest technologies and unusual fabrics. One piece featured crazy-quilt blocks made entirely of fabric, zippers, elastic, laces and garters from old corsets. The smallest quilt was less than ten inches square, while the largest stretched ten feet in one direction and eight feet in the other.

Quilt National '87 included the work of four men who proved that quiltmaking was no longer the exclusive domain of women. One of the '87 quilts reached a new dimension—a third dimension. Quilt artist Virginia Jacobs slipped an eight-foot balloon into a quilted cover and inflated it with a blowing vacuum cleaner. The result was a huge quilted ball resting on its own "nest" of coiled quilted rope. Another piece had pleats which stood away from the surface and changed from shades of black and gray to reds, blues and greens as the viewer's glance moved from one edge of the quilt to the other.

Recognizing that the majority of quilts in a Dairy Barn installation would be suspended from the ceiling, several of the '87 exhibitors made two-sided quilts which gave the visitors even more to see. Many of the quilts were adorned with non-fabric elements such as baskets, buttons, beads, stuffed figures, feathers, jewelry and plastic leaves.

Visitors to Quilt National '89 will no doubt remember it as the year of "quilt plus object." Artists are now including additional objects—unattached to the quilted surface—as part of their work. The chair with Elizabeth Busch's work and the vase with Terrie Mangat's are integral elements in their statements. The collection includes many names which are quite familiar to Quilt National visitors, but the majority of the artists are new to this series of exhibits.

It has been an exciting decade marked by change and challenge. The art quiltmakers of the '80s have satisfied their creative energies, and in so doing have enriched us all by providing an enormous body of work which adds to the heritage begun generations ago.

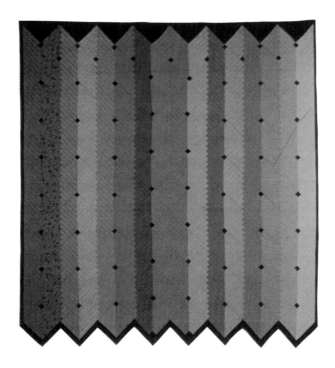

The following pages contain a sampling of works from Quilt National '79 and '81, for which catalogs are no longer available. The complete '83, '85 and '87 collections are documented in other volumes published by and available from Schiffer Publishers.

Virginia Randles
Fences—
Cotton fabrics. Machine pieced and hand quilted.
78" x 82" (QN '79)

Judi Warren
Hot Mobius
Cotton fabrics. Machine pieced and hand quilted.
71" x 71" (QN '81)

Jan Myers
Beulahland
Hand-dyed cottons. Machine pieced and hand quilted.
42" x 46" (QN '81)

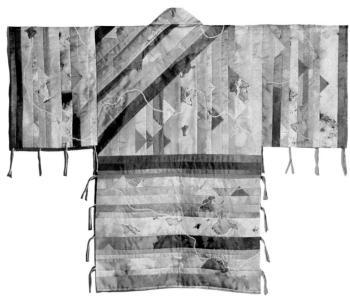

Yvonne Porcella
A World Beyond the Clouds
Hand-dyed silk. Machine pieced, hand
quilted and beaded.
48″ x 36″ folded (QN '81)

Judy Mathieson
Floating City
Cotton fabrics. Hand and machine pieced,
hand quilted.
62″ x 67″ (QN '81)

Nancy Halpern
Hilltown
Cottons and blends. Machine pieced and
hand quilted.
71″ x 73″ (QN '81)

Paula Lederkramer
Bits & Pieces
Cottons and blends. Hand pieced and hand quilted.
60" x 80" (QN '81)

Marie Shirer
French Knot
Cottons and blends. Hand pieced and hand quilted.
57" x 57" (QN '81)

Judith Dingle
Windows
Cottons and cotton blends.
80" x 84" (QN '81)

Carolyn G. Muller
Self Portrait of a Quiltmaker
Cotton, velveteen, moire, chintz, satin and netting.
47″ x 54″ (QN '81)

Jean Hewes
The Striped Lady
Cotton, rayon, linen and synthetics. Machine appliquéd and quilted.
42″ x 76″ (QN '81)

Sister Linda Fowler
P.C.
Silk-screened cotton.
67″ x 98″ (QN '81)

Judith Larzelere
Marriage of Blue & Orange
Cotton Fabrics. Machine pieced and quilted.
108" x 76" (QN '81)

Nell Cogswell
Cape Porpoise Quilt
Cottons and blends. Hand appliquéd and
embroidered, hand quilted.
96" x 108" (QN '79)

Maria McCormick-Snyder
Mirage
Cotton fabrics. Machine pieced and hand
quilted.
60" x 60" (QN '81)

Joyce Marquess Carey
Puzzle Quilt
Velveteen, satin and buttons. Pieced units can
be rearranged.
84″ x 84″ (QN '79)

Mirjana Ugrinov
Paper Quilt I
Assorted materials. Machine pieced.
29″ x 62″ (QN '79)

Rosalie Lamanna
Warm Watergate Coverup
Cotton, wool roving and wool challis.
Machine pieced and hand quilted.
51″ x 63″ (QN '79)

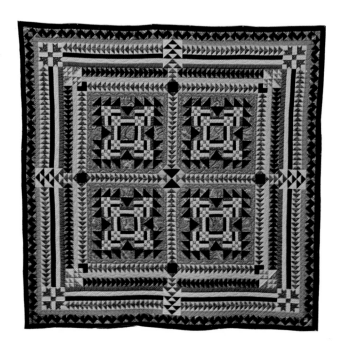

Chris Wolf Edmonds
Fox and Geese
Cotton fabrics. Hand pieced and hand quilted.
64″ x 64″ (QN '79)

Patsy Allen
Nine Squares
Fabric and ribbon. Machine pieced and quilted.
32″ x 30″ (QN '81)

Rhoda Cohen
Maine Quilt
Cottons and blends. Machine pieced, hand appliquéd, machine quilted in strips.
60″ x 108″ (QN '79)

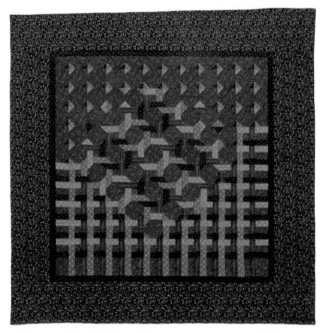

Nancy Crow
February Study I
Cottons and blends. Machine pieced and strip
pieced; hand quilted by Velma Brill.
48″ x 48″ (QN '79)

Pamela Gustavson Johnson
Chains and Bands
Cotton fabrics. Machine pieced and hand
quilted.
50″ x 50″ (QN '79)

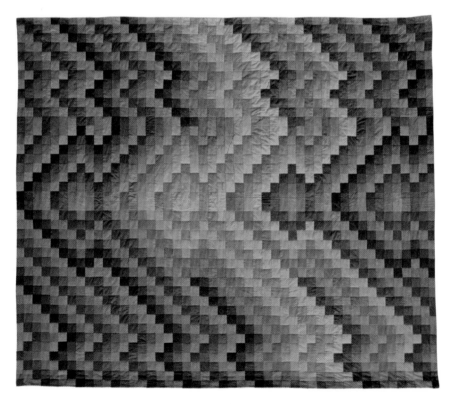

Debra Millard-Lunn
Counterpoint
Cotton fabrics. Machine pieced and hand
quilted.
92″ x 76″ (QN '79)

Michael James
Dawn Nebula
Cotton, satin and velveteen. Hand pieced and
hand quilted.
48″ x 54″ (QN '79)

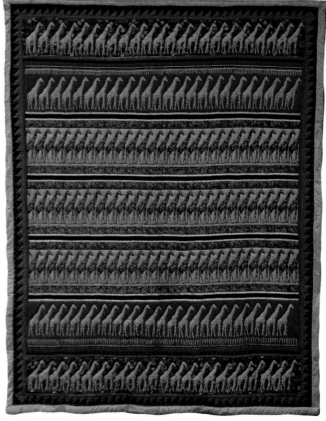

Françoise Barnes
Etudes de Courbes
Cotton fabrics. Machine pieced and hand
quilted.
73″ x 75″ (QN '79)

Terrie H. Mangat
Giraffes
Cotton fabrics. Hand quilted.
86″ x 96″ (QN '79)

Index to Quilt National 1979-1989

During its first decade Quilt National has featured 468 works by 264 different artists. The following is a listing of all the artists and works which have been included in the current and past Quilt National exhibits.

Images of many of the works from Quilt National '79 and '81 may be found in *The New American Quilt* (Fiberarts/Lark publications, 1981.) Quilt National '83 is documented in *THE QUILT: New Directions for an American Tradition* (Schiffer Publishing, 1983.) *QUILTS: The State of an Art* (Schiffer Publishing, 1985) and *FIBER EXPRESSIONS: The Contemporary Quilt* (Schiffer Publishing, 1987) include photographs of all of the works in Quilt National '85 and '87.

A

Accardi, Carolyn
Untitled #1 ('85)
Adams, Ann
Polyfest ('89)
Albert, Judith Greene
Rabbit Transit ('81)
Allen, Patsy
Blue Trapezium ('81)
Nine Squares ('81)
Deco Series #2 ('83)
Deco Pinwheel VI: Threshold ('89)
Alvarez, Sue
Tennessee Ribbons ('85)
That's the Way It Goes... ('89)
Anderson, Faye
*Astral Macaroni with Blueberry
    Vinaigrette* ('85)
Volatile Material ('85)
Anderson, Gerlinde
Flamingos Along the Shore ('83)
Anderson, Virginia
Linkage ('79)
Whirligig ('79)
Anthony, Janice
Great Wall of China ('83)
Avery, Virginia
Leftover Lilies ('85)

B

Baker, Carol
Reference Work ('79)
Barnes, Françoise
Etudes de Courbes ('79)
Eyes of Isis ('79)
Untitled ('83)
Inhibitions 16 ('85)
S.A.M.Y. ('85)
Misumena Ellipsoides ('87)
Bartlett, Roxana
*Return/The Dreams That Wolf-Dog
    Told Me* ('87)
Wild Snow Chase ('89)
Beals, Virginia Allaire
One Moon Rising ('81)
Rose Mirage ('83)

Becker, Judy
African Rhythms ('89)
Benner, Sue
Summer ('89)
Bennett, Robin Corthell
Confetti ('87)
Berner, Julie Roach
Southwestern Festival ('81)
One Fine Day ('85)
Bero, Mary
Dream Dazzler ('83)
Bird, Ann
Blue Star ('81)
Dancers ('81)
Blair, Jane
Parcheesi ('85)
Summer ('87)
Boyd, Mary Petrina
Change Ringing ('87)
Brainard, Katherine
Zebra Quilt ('87)
Broadwell, Sally
Goose Crossing ('85)
Brown, Tafi
Heller's Quilt ('79)
Deer Knoll Dairy I ('81)
Trees IV: All Seasons ('89)
Büchel, Uta and **Ellen Harlizius-Klück**
Weather-beaten Roof ('89)
Buck, Christina
Medallion ('79)
Starlit Night ('79)
Burbidge, Pauline
Cubic Log Cabin ('83)-**Award of
    Excellence**
Cubic Pyramid ('83)-**Award of
    Excellence**
Finn ('85)
Diagonal Zig-Zag ('87)
Still Life Quilt I ('87)
Burg, Pamela Jean
Curtain ('81)-**Best of Show Award**
Terry's Cloth ('83)
Burian, Ann and **Ruth Zachary**
The Magic Carpet ('83)

Burke, Janie
Fruit Slices Quilt ('81)
Rainbow Sherbets Quilt ('81)
Busch, Elizabeth A.
Haystack Sunrise ('85)
Child Dream ('89)
When We Were Young ('89)-**Best of
    Show Award**

C

Campbell, Christine
*Chapter IX, The Pioneer Women, from
    Willa Cather's My Antonia* ('85)
Carabas, Leslie
On an Expressionistic Theme ('81)
Chairs ('87)
Carey, Joyce Marquess
Puzzle Quilt ('79)
Tesselated Twill ('83)
Glad Rags ('89)
Carlson, Nedra
Follow the Yellow Brick Road ('83)
Casey, Kathi
Night Chasms ('87)
Chaffee, Marilyn McKenzie
Del Rio Quilt ('83)
Clark, Sharon Johnson
Ins and Outs ('89)
Claybrook, Marjorie
The Amish Toucan ('83)
Cochran, Jane Burch
Ceremonial Cloth: Zuni Roses ('87)
Crazy Quilt for a Half-Breed ('87)
*Phases of the Heart, Phases of
    the Moon* ('89)
Cogswell, Nell
Cape Porpoise Quilt ('79)
Cody, Pat
Deco Diamonds ('83)
Cohen, Rhoda
Here Comes the Sun ('79)
Maine Quilt ('79)
Coleman, Lisa
Hickety-Pickety ('83)
Combs, Marie
Refractions on a Black Field ('81)

Coole, Margaret S.
Double Green Glazing ('83)
Crane, Barbara Lydecker
Internal Map ('89)
Crasco, Nancy
Lauren's Rainbow Quilt ('79)
Crow, Nancy
February Study I ('79)
February Study II ('79)
January Study II ('79)
Bittersweet XIII ('81)
Tramp Art I ('83)
Passion ('85)
Mexican Wheels I ('89)
Cullinan, Benita
This Isn't Cleveland ('79)
Cunha, Rhonda
Blue Loops ('83)
Cuppini, Pamela Breuckner
Untitled ('79)

D

Dales, Judy B.
Pale Reflections ('83)
Davis, Ardyth
Aurora II ('83)
Tied Bars/Mauve-Jade ('85)-**Award of Excellence**
Tied Bars/Red-Blue ('85)-**Award of Excellence**
Horizon I/Blue ('89)
Devore, Mary Jane
Morning Glory ('81)
DeWitt, Rita
She Had Strange Dreams Whenever She Wore Her Grandmother's Nightcap ('81)
Too Many Airbrushed Smiles ('85)
Dingle, Judith
Windows ('81)
Reconstruction ('89)-**Award for Most Innovative Use of the Medium**
Donnell, Radka
Earth, Water, Air and Fire ('79)
The Plumage of the Ascending Goddess ('85)

Dorman, Patrick
Revelation ('87)-**Award of Excellence**

E

Edmonds, Chris Wolf
Fox and Geese ('79)
Night Rainbow: A Place for Everything and Everything in Its Place ('83)
Partitions II ('85)
Symmetry P2GG ('87)
Left-Handed Compliments ('89)
Einstein, Sylvia H.
Saturday Night in the Park ('85)
Charivari ('87)
Elvgren, Betty Jo
The Twelve Days of Christmas ('83)-**People's Choice Award**
Engle, Lauren
Litho Quilt ('81)
Enright, Zoe
Great Peaches ('83)
Erickson, Nancy
Jupiter Watch over Capybaraland ('83)
The Visitation ('89)

F

Fallert, Carol Bryer
High Tech Tucks ('87)
Farling, Kathleen M.
Indigo and Shibori Quilt with Kanoko Dots ('83)
Fay, Liz Alpert
The Silent Trooper ('85)
..A Letter from Arthur ('87)
Felix, Deborah
Prisoner of the Garden ('85)
Bob in the Bathtub ('87)
Paper Faces ('87)
Fishing for the Intangible ('89)
Finch-Hurley, Jerri
Wind ('87)
Fitzgerald, Veronica
Untitled ('85)-**Best of Show Award**
Fouts, Linda
Family Quilt ('81)

Fowler, Sister Linda
P.C. ('81)
Fritz, Laura Lee
And Crown Her Good With Brotherhood ('87)-**Domini McCarthy Award for Exceptional Craftsmanship /co-recipient**
Frosch, Suzanna
Helenic Heritage I, II & III ('85)
Fuhr, Alex
Untitled ('85)
Quilt ('87)
Fujishiro, Ikuko
Flower in Full Bloom ('87)
A Burning Heart ('89)

G

Gerber-Senger, Ursula
Polarity ('89)
Gersen, Carol H.
Bonnema Bedquilt ('85)
Thinking of Winter ('85)
The Greens of Summer ('87)
Chinese Coins Variation: Skylines ('89)
Giddens, Helen
Armadillo Highway ('89)
Gilfert, Sara
Japanese Silk Calendar Quilt: Concealment/Revealment Series II ('81)
Giordano, JoAnn
Ideal Love Mate Shrines ('85)
Gipple, Nancy
Score for Bluegrass Sewing Machine ('81)
Cedar Box Fans ('83)
Rock Garden for Donald and Verdell ('87)
Glover, Flavin
Farmstead ('83)
Green, Casey
Kaleidoscope ('83)
Gribble, Carol
Paper Patchwork ('81)
Grier, Karen
Painted Bunting ('83)

Gurrier, Elizabeth
Fragments ('87)
Gutcheon, Beth
Lost City ('79)

H

Haines, Maryellen
Minimal One ('83)
Hajzl, Donna
Paper Quilt ('81)
Halpern, Nancy
Flying Carpet ('79)
Hilltown ('81)
Maple Leaf Rag ('85)-**Domini McCarthy Award for Exceptional Craftsmanship /co-recipient**
Landfall ('87)
Anemone Rag ('89)
Hanson, Gail A.
Be the First to Get Your Marbles Home ('83)
Hartman, Barbara Oliver
Safari Blizzard ('89)
Harlizius-Klück, Ellen
see **Büchel**
Hawkins, Patty
Cactus People ('89)
Hearst, Judy Wasserman
Garden of the Indulgent Delight ('85)
Heidingsfelder, Sharon
Melody in Color ('85)
Almost a Melody ('87)
Encore, Encore ('89)
Herman, Nancy
Poppies III ('85)
Herrold, Anneke
Craziness Behind the Fence ('87)
Hewes, Jean
Red-Gold Man ('81)-**Award for Most Innovative Use of the Medium**
The Sitter ('81)-**Award for Most Innovative Use of the Medium**
The Striped Lady ('81)-**Award for Most Innovative Use of the Medium**
Pillars ('83)-**Domini McCarthy Award for Exceptional Craftsmanship**

Sticks ('83)-**Domini McCarthy Award for Exceptional Craftsmanship**
Rocketing ('85)
Holmstrand, Bonnie Bucknam
These Raindrops are Rosie's Fault ('87)
Holst, Christine
Watching T. V. ('83)
Hornung, David
Big Blue ('81)-**Award of Excellence**
Object, Shape and Symbol ('81)-**Award of Excellence**
Pictorial Arrangement ('81)-**Award of Excellence**
The Nile ('85)
Hoskin, Sharla Jean
Triptych ('79)
Hueber, Inge
Reflected Image ('87)
Diabolo ('89)
Humberson, Sandra
Star Map ('83)
Hungerland, Buff
Auras & Edges ('83)
Huyck, Marion L.
Russian Medallion ('83)

I

Iddings, Treva J.
Necktie Dahlias ('81)
Ingram-Bartholomäus, Bridget
Islamic Inspiration ('87)
Untitled ('87)
Irvine, Jan
Elipse II ('89)

J

Jackson, Damaris
Lines from the Park ('87)
Jacobs, Laurie
"...but there was a faulty joint in the right rocket booster." ('87)
Hen Party ('87)
Jacobs, Teresa Cooper
Through the Hourglass (or Big Bo Peep) ('89)

Jacobs, Virginia
Sky Quilts ('81)
IFQ83-Magic Carpet ('83)
Krakow Kabuki Waltz ('87)-**Award for Most Innovative Use of the Medium**
James, Michael
Dawn Nebula ('79)
Rhythmetron ('81)
Strip Quilt No. 4: Candylily ('81)
Untitled Strip No. 5 ('81)
La Tempete ('83)
Bias Cut ('87)
Janke-Weber, Lynette
Untitled ('79)
Jensen, Margot Strand
Coming Unglued ('85)
Harlequinade ('85)
Jessen, Carol
Ice Cream Parlor Chairs ('89)
Johnson, Pamela Gustavson
Chains and Bands ('79)
Log Cabin: 4 Corners/Contrasts ('83)
Yellow Square II ('85)
Black and White Log Cabin ('87)
Joslyn, Catherine
Pieced Quilt '80: Dreamscape ('81)
Akan Tribute ('83)
Joyal, Pat
Fredrique ('85)
Joyce, Ann
Ex Libris ('89)
Junker, Holley
Flowerseed Farm ('85)-**Award for Most Innovative Use of the Medium /co-recipient**
Infrared River Valley ('87)
Q'est Seurat? Seurat! ('89)

K

Kahmann, Irene
Captured Light ('89)
Kamm, Rebecca
Quilted Ocean Park ('85)

Katz, Donna J.
  Dragonfly Paper ('83)
  Flower Bed ('85)
Keller, Carol
  Radiance ('79)
  Twilight ('85)
Kawaguchi, Kaoru
  Nagareru ('89)
Kempers-Cullen, Natasha
  Daydream at Dusk ('89)
King, Glenda
  LCC 2:3 ('89)
Kjelland, Suzanne
  RainGlow ('81)
Klein, Jody
  Cows Grazing Along the Milky Way ('79)
  Quilt for Outstanding Homonculus Motorcycle Riders ('81)
  108 Cows with Silver Tails ('83)
Knauer, Katherine
  Air Force ('87)
  Planet X Comix ('89)
Koons, Nancy
  Sea Dreams ('79)
Kowaleski, Ann
  Masked Oaxacan Stilt Dancers ('89)
Kristoferson, Susan
  Counting Forty-Six ('81)

L

Labbens, Soizik
  Oh! Happy Days! ('85)
Lamanna, Rosalie
  Warm Watergate Coverup ('79)
Lambert, Cynthia and **Janet Lorini**
  St. Irving and the Archangels ('89)
Larzelere, Judith
  Marriage of Blue & Orange ('81)
  Summer ('83)
  Red/Blue Jar ('85)
  Sunrise: Jappa Flat ('87)
  Chains of Blood, Tears of Rust ('89)
Lederkramer, Paula
  Bits & Pieces ('81)
Lee, Susan Webb
  Mozambique ('87)

Lefferdink, Virginia
  Rain and Shine ('83)
Levin, Linda
  A Clear Day and No Memories ('85)
  What You Remember is Saved ('87)
  Pallone: Siena Di Mattina ('89)
Lintault, M. Joan
  Heavenly Bodies ('81)
  Journey to the Mountains ('81)
Lizon, Tana Krizova
  Space I ('83)
Loeb, Emiko Toda
  Taketorimonogatari ("The Bamboo Cutter" Folktale) ('89)
Lorini, Janet
  see **Lambert**

M

MacDonald, Linda
  Dusk, 1981 ('81)
  Ruth Fresno's Dream ('83)
  Shooting Gallery ('85)
  Chasing Red Dogs ('87)
  Salmon Ladders ('87)
  Weaving Zebra Dancers ('89)
Macey, Barbara
  Red Quilt ('85)
Maher, Jan
  Reflections IV ('89)
Malarcher, Patricia
  Detour ('89)
Malwitz, Marguerite
  Desert Dusk ('89)
Mangat, Terrie Hancock
  Charolais Cows ('79)
  Giraffes ('79)
  Covington Slickers: Rainy Days in Cincinnati ('81)
  Fishing Hats over Rose Lake ('83)·**Award for Most Innovative Use of the Medium**
  Sunny Day on Cochina Beach ('83)
  Lightning Runners ('85)
  Shrine to the Beginning ('89)
  Sky Stones ('89)

Martin, Jeanne
  Untitled ('89)
Mason, Merrill
  Tornado I ('89)
Mathieson, Judy
  Norman Wall ('79)
  Floating City ('81)
  Nautical Stars ('87)·**Domini McCarthy Award for Exceptional Craftsmanship /co-recipient People's Choice Award,**
May, Therese
  Monster Quilt ('83)
  God Bless Us, One and All ('85)·**Award for Most Innovative Use of the Medium /co-recipient**
  Saw Blade ('85)·**Award for Most Innovative Use of the Medium /co-recipient**
  Fish and Chicks ('87)
  Rose ('89)
McCann, Marianne
  Heffer and Peffer ('87)
McCluskey, Robin A.
  Tiger Claw ('81)
McCormick-Snyder, Maria
  Labyrinth ('79)
  Log Cabin Variation ('79)
  Mirage ('81)
McDowell, Ruth B.
  Bee Balm—Monarda Didyma ('81)
  Lady's Mantle—Alchemilla Vulgaris ('81)
  Luna Moths ('83)
  Geraniums ('85)
  Meadow Saffron ('87)
  The Yellow Maple ('89)
McKeever, Kathy Hall
  T.R.I.X. ('85)
Melody, Marion
  Rondo of Life ('85)
Messier, W. Kim Chee
  Farmyard Composition ('83)
  NYCity ('87)
Meyer, Megan Walters
  Woven Illusions ('81)

Millard-Lunn, Debra
Counterpoint ('79)
Ice Flows ('81)
Penta Squares ('83)
Plains Geometry ('87)
Miller, Margaret
Melon Patch ('85)
Rolling Thunder ('87)
Miyatani, Machiko
Fantasy I ("85)
Morgan, Mary
Diffraction II ('87)
Number 30 ('87)
Mortenson, Barbara J.
Breaking Loose ("87)
Muller, Carolyn G.
Another Day ('79)
Red Door Quilt ('79)
Self Portrait of a Quiltmaker ('81)
Murphy, Susan Kolojeski
Wrappers ('79)
Murray, Clare M.
Travelog #1: Aldstadt ('89)
Murray, Karen Lynn
Transition ('83)
Myers, Sharon
Wauwinet Sky ('83)
Myers-Newbury, Jan
Anemone ('81)
Beulahland ('81)
Galaxial Four-Patch ('85)
Morning Glory ('87)
Night Swarm ('89)

N

Nagin, Risë '
Forty-Eight Triangles ('85)
*Tunnel Vision: Henri Matisse at Blue
    Mountain* ('85)
Road Goliaths ('87)
Sights in Transit ('87)

Nathan Roberts, Miriam
Kyoto ('83)
Lattice Interweave ('85)·**People's
    Choice Award**
Nancy's Fancy ('85)
Letting Go ('89)
The Museum ('89)
Niesner, Liesel
"...ein Regenbogen für GREENPEACE."
    ('89)·**Domini McCarthy Award
    for Exceptional Craftsmanship**
Newbill, Elizabeth
Squaredance ('85)
Nixon, Joy
On the Line ('83)
Nixon-Hudson, Cynthia
Floating Isadora I & II ('79)
Melinda's Window ('81)
Noble, Carol Rasmussen
Pinwheel Pavement ('79)

O

Oliver, Connie
Folk Triptych ('83)
Revenge of the Scrolls ('87)
O'Neil, Elaine
Memory Garden ('85)
Oppenheimer, Ellen
*The Quilt That's Supposed to Be on Our
    Bed* ('83)
Zoe's Quilt ('85)
Broken Arm Quilt ('87)
New Year's Eve Party ('89)

P

Packer, Barbara
Interrupted Forward Progress ('83)
Rainbow Interweave ('83)
Page-Kessler, Janet
Windmills of My Mind ('85)
Still Life V/VI ('89)
Parker, Kay
Whales and Snails ('83)

Parkhurst, Esther
Four Corners ('81)
Joseph's Coat ('83)
Connections II ('87)
The Great Divide ('87)
Black & White with Raw Edges ('89)
Partee, Cherry
The Epiphany of Joanna Burden ('89)
Long Distance Call ('89)
Pasquini, Katie
Kiro-Shiro ('87)
Perry, Linda S.
Thoughts of Karen ('89)
Pfaff, Julia E.
*Greek Geometry in Black,
    Green & Blue* ('87)
Phillips, Sherry
Medallion ('79)
Plogman, Elaine
Magnolia Quilt ('79)
Off To See the Wizard ('85)
Winter Storm Warning ('87)
Porcella, Yvonne
Takoage ('81)
A World Beyond the Clouds ('81)
Floating World ('83)
Robe for a Dragonrider ('83)
When All the Colors Come Dancing ('85)
*Taking the Greyhound to
    Bakersfield* ('87)
Riding an 8 Legged Camel ('89)
Prentice, Dinah
Perspective Drawing ('83)
Hermeneutics ('85)

R

Randles, Virginia
Fences—('79)
Sundown ('81)
Rankin, Ann
*Batik Block and Screen
    Printed Quilt* ('79)
Reeves, Jane
Windhover I ('83)
Post Modern XIII ('89)

Rhode, Ann
Basket Bazaar ('85)
Rhodes, Sara Long
Indian Blanket ('83)
Understanding Each Other ('85)
National Cohesion ('87)
Robinson, Sharon
Equis Robis I ('79)
Equis Robis II ('79)
Hanging Quilt IV ('79)
Untitled Green Blanket ('81)
Romey, Lucretia
Diagonal Barns ('83)
Ross, Lynne
Seasons Series; Spring Lilies ('85)
Rothstein, Lynn Last
Black Cheeked Man with Wrinkles ('87)

S

Sage, Linda Karel
A Floosier Hoosier ('85)
Sassaman, Jane A.
Zig-Zag Spiral ('89)
Saville, Joy
Time Warp ('81)
Dance of Chi ('89)
Scadden, Andrea Leong
Night Flight ('83)
Schaefer, Becky
Requiem ('87)
Schlotzhauer, Joyce
Attic Layaways ('87)
Schroeder, Susan
#1 ('81)
#2 ('81)
Schulze, Joan
Old Koi, Old Pond ('89)
Schwalb, Robin
Let X=X ('87)
*PCB Bop ('89)·**Award of Excellence***
Rosetta Stone ('89)
Seigel, Rebekka
Duck Pond ('83)
Sharpe, Susan
Family Photo Album ('79)

Shie, Susan
*Neighborhood with Comet Scar ('87)·**Best**
of Show Award
Tropical New York ('89)
Shirer, Marie
French Knot ('81)
Silk, Louise
City Quilts III ('87)
Smiler, Ruth
Matrix II ('81)
Matrix III ('83)
Smith, Lori Barraco
Brugh Na Boinne ('85)
Smith, Margorie Whitehall
October ('79)
Smith, Mary Lou
Williamsburg Garden ('81)
Light in the Forest ('83)
Smith, Suma
Primary Fantasy ('89)
Soesemann, Petra
Coffee Cups ('85)
Garden ('85)
Ideas for Topiary: Carnivorous
Garden ('87)
Sonobe, Michiko
Café Bar ('87)
Vakansu ('87)
Spaeth, Peggy
Boxes and Stars ('79)
Dodecagons ('83)
Foldings ('85)
Squares and Stars ('87)
Speakes, Rebecca
HeatWave ('89)
Spears, Jeanie May
Passages ('79)
Delectable Mountains Dreamed ('83)
Stader, Donna
Antigua ('87)
Starr, Claire
In Celebration ('85)
Stern-Straeter, Dorle
Blue Kaleidoscope ('81)
Lotus ('81)
Arabia, ('89)

Stothers, Marilyn
Curving Cubes ('85)
Strider, Margie
Farm Fantasy Patches ('79)
Strother, Debra Turner
Great Blue Herons ('87)
Studstill, Pam
*Quilt #21 ('83)·**Best of Show Award***
*Quilt #22 ('83)·**Best of Show Award***
Sudo, Kumiko
Revelation ('87)
Swan, Julia
The Raggedy Men ('87)

T

Taskey, Jan Taylor
Red Alert ('85)
Thornton, Bonnie J.
The Turquoise Trail ('87)
Tolliver, Carolyn
Margins ('83)
Trent, Sue
Corset Quilt ('85)
Trichler, Nan
Black Cherry Swirl ('83)
Africa ('85)
Tamiami Trail ('85)

U

Ugrinov, Mirjana
Paper Quilt I ('79)
Paper Quilt II ('79)
Usilton, Darcy
Blessed Darcy Taming ('87)
Putting the Guise to Bed ('89)

V

Vincil, Priscilla
Barred Fantasy ('81)
Von Weise, Wenda F.
Fabricated Landscape:
Straight Furrows ('79)
Fabricated Landscape: Shifted Geologic
Strata ('81)
Fabricated Cityscape: Stadium Day ('83)

W

Walker, David
  Centersearch ('87)
  The Enchanted Land
    of the Lotus Eaters ('89)
  Renascence for Rebecca ('89)
Walker, Michele
  Aquarius ('87)
Walker, Paul Wesley
  Stairway to Heaven ('81)
Wallis, Lucy
  Circle on Square ('85)
Warren, Judi
  Art Deco: Making Z's ('81)
  Hot Mobius ('81)
  Interior/Exterior Windowscape: Grass
    and Glass ('83)
  Santa Fe: Sky Ceremony ('85)
  Blossoms and Breaks ('87)
  March 28, 1986: Rain at Fushimi Inari
    ('89)
Westfall, Carol D.
  Crazy Quilt I ('89)
Whittington, Nancy
  Leaf Symmetry I ('87)
Winzenz, Karen Hagermeister
  Quilt Progression: Fading ('79)
Wise, Susan
  Delectable Mountains ('79)
Woringer, Anne
  Urubamba ('87)
Wujcik, Beverly
  Marooned ('81)

Z

Zachary, Ruth
  see **Burian**
Zopf, Emily
  Water Music ('89)

Index

A

Adams, Ann
Polyfest, page 32
Allen, Patsy
Deco Pinwheel VI: Threshold, page 73
Nine Squares, page 85
Alvarez, Sue
That's the Way It Goes..., page 58

B

Barnes, Françoise
Etudes de Courbes, page 87
Bartlett, Roxana
Wild Snow Chase, page 44
Becker, Judy
African Rhythms, page 52
Benner, Sue
Summer, page 25
Brown, Tafi
Trees IV: All Seasons, page 15
Büchel, Uta and **Ellen Harlizius-Klück**
Weather-beaten Roof, page 33
Busch, Elizabeth A.
Child Dream, page 51
When We Were Young, page 59

C

Carey, Joyce Marquess
Glad Rags, page 73
Puzzle Quilt, page 84
Clark, Sharon Johnson
Ins and Outs, page 22
Cochran, Jane Burch
Phases of the Heart, Phases of the Moon, page 28
Cogswell, Nell
Cape Porpoise Quilt, page 83
Cohen, Rhoda
Maine Quilt, page 85
Crane, Barbara Lydecker
Internal Map, page 22
Crow, Nancy
February Study I, page 86
Mexican Wheels I, page 31

D

Davis, Ardyth
Horizon I/Blue, page 36
Dingle, Judith
Reconstruction, page 10
Windows, page 81

E

Edmonds, Chris Wolf
Fox and Geese, page 85
Left-Handed Compliments, page 70
Erickson, Nancy
The Visitation, page 17

F

Felix, Deborah
Fishing for the Intangible, page 34
Fowler, Sister Linda
P.C., page 82
Fujishiro, Ikuko
A Burning Heart, page 56

G

Gerber-Senger, Ursula
Polarity, page 43
Gersen, Carol H.
Chinese Coins Variation: Skylines, page 63
Giddens, Helen
Armadillo Highway, page 64

H

Halpern, Nancy
Anemone Rag, page 40
Hilltown, page 80
Hartman, Barbara Oliver
Safari Blizzard, page 11
Harlizius-Klück, Ellen
see **Büchel**
Hawkins, Patty
Cactus People, page 68
Heidingsfelder, Sharon
Encore, Encore, page 25
Hueber, Inge
Diabolo, page 55

Hewes, Jean
The Striped Lady, page 82

I

Irvine, Jan
Elipse II, page 38

J

Jacobs, Teresa Cooper
Through the Hourglass (or Big Bo Peep), page 54
James, Michael
Dawn Nebula, page 87
Jessen, Carol
Ice Cream Parlor Chairs, page 24
Johnson, Pamela Gustavson
Chains and Bands, page 86
Joyce, Ann
Ex Libris, page 60
Junker, Holley
Q'est Seurat? Seurat!, page 50

K

Kahmann, Irene
Captured Light, page 16
Kawaguchi, Kaoru
Nagareru, page 23
Kempers-Cullen, Natasha
Daydream at Dusk, page 18
King, Glenda
LCC 2:3, page 52
Knauer, Katherine
Planet X Comix, page 41
Kowaleski, Ann
Masked Oaxacan Stilt Dancers, page 65

L

Lamanna, Rosalie
Warm Watergate Coverup, page 84
Lambert, Cynthia and **Janet Lorini**
St. Irving and the Archangels, page 55
Larzelere, Judith
Chains of Blood, Tears of Rust, page 37
Marriage of Blue & Orange, page 83
Lederkramer, Paula
Bits & Pieces, page 81

Levin, Linda
  Pallone: Siena Di Mattina, page 43
Loeb, Emiko Toda
  *Taketorimonogatari ("The Bamboo
  Cutter" Folktale)*, page 21
Lorini, Janet
  see **Lambert**

M

MacDonald, Linda
  Weaving Zebra Dancers, page 41
Maher, Jan
  Reflections IV, page 11
Malarcher, Patricia
  Detour, page 32
Malwitz, Marguerite
  Desert Dusk, page 17
Mangat, Terrie H.
  Giraffes, page 87
  Shrine to the Beginning, page 30
  Sky Stones, page 46
Martin, Jeanne
  Untitled, page 49
Mason, Merrill
  Tornado I, page 37
Mathieson, Judy
  Floating City, page 80
May, Therese
  Rose, page 29
McCormick-Snyder, Maria
  Mirage, page 83
McDowell, Ruth B.
  The Yellow Maple, page 12
Millard-Lunn, Debra
  Counterpoint, page 86
Muller, Carolyn G.
  Self Portrait of a Quiltmaker, page 82
Murray, Clare M.
  Travelog #1: Aldstadt, page 69
Myers-Newbury, Jan
  Beulahland, page 79
  Night Swarm, page 63

N

Nathan Roberts, Miriam
  Letting Go, page 61
  The Museum, page 61
Niesner, Liesel
  "...ein Regenbogen für GREENPEACE.",
  page 39

O

Oppenheimer, Ellen
  New Year's Eve Party, page 65

P

Page-Kessler, Janet
  Still Life V/VI, page 72
Parkhurst, Esther
  Black & White with Raw Edges, page 42
Partee, Cherry
  Long Distance Call, page 66
  The Epiphany of Joanna Burden, page 62
Perry, Linda S.
  Thoughts of Karen, page 19
Porcella, Yvonne
  Riding an 8 Legged Camel, page 71
  A World Beyond the Clouds, page 80

R

Randles, Virginia
  Fences—, page 79
Reeves, Jane
  Post Modern XIII, page 15

S

Sassaman, Jane A.
  Zig-Zag Spiral, page 53
Saville, Joy
  Dance of Chi, page 45
Schulze, Joan
  Old Koi, Old Pond, page 14
Schwalb, Robin
  PCB Bop, page 35
  Rosetta Stone, page 49

Shie, Susan
  Tropical New York, page 26
Shirer, Marie
  French Knot, page 81
Smith, Suma
  Primary Fantasy, page 67
Speakes, Rebecca
  HeatWave, page 68
Stern-Straeter, Dorle
  Arabia, page 13

U

Ugrinov, Mirjana
  Paper Quilt I, page 84
Usilton, Darcy
  Putting the Guise to Bed, page 47

W

Walker, David
  *The Enchanted Land of
  the Lotus Eaters*, page 27
  Renascence for Rebecca, page 74
Warren, Judi
  Hot Mobius, page 79
  *March 28, 1986: Rain at Fushimi
  Inari*, page 57
Westfall, Carol D.
  Crazy Quilt I, page 20

Z

Zopf, Emily
  Water Music, page 48